Elena Trost

Social Media Marketing in BRIC Countries

Internet Economics
Internetökonomie

edited by
herausgegeben von

Prof. Dr. Julia Maintz
(Cologne Business School (CBS) –
European University of Applied Sciences)

Volume / Band 6

LIT

Elena Trost

Social Media Marketing in BRIC Countries

Examining case studies of BMW, adidas and NIVEA

LIT

This book is printed on acid-free paper.

Bibliographic information published by the Deutsche Nationalbibliothek
The Deutsche Nationalbibliothek lists this publication in the Deutsche Nationalbibliografie; detailed bibliographic data are available in the Internet at http://dnb.d-nb.de.

ISBN 978-3-643-90264-1

A catalogue record for this book is available from the British Library

Klosbachstr. 107
CH-8032 Zürich
Tel. +41 (0) 44-251 75 05
Fax +41 (0) 44-251 75 06
E-Mail: zuerich@lit-verlag.ch
http://www.lit-verlag.ch

LIT VERLAG Dr. W. Hopf
Berlin 2013
Fresnostr. 2
D-48159 Münster
Tel. +49 (0) 2 51-62 03 20
Fax +49 (0) 2 51-23 19 72
E-Mail: lit@lit-verlag.de
http://www.lit-verlag.de

Distribution:
In Germany: LIT Verlag Fresnostr. 2, D-48159 Münster
Tel. +49 (0) 2 51-620 32 22, Fax +49 (0) 2 51-922 60 99, E-mail: vertrieb@lit-verlag.de

In Austria: Medienlogistik Pichler-ÖBZ, e-mail: mlo@medien-logistik.at
In the UK: Global Book Marketing, e-mail: mo@centralbooks.com
In North America: International Specialized Book Services, e-mail: orders@isbs.com
e-books are available at www.litwebshop.de

Für meine Familie, Friederike und Idgy

&

Susanne, Oliver und Burak

Information about the author

Elena Trost introduces the connection of social media marketing and the fastest growing countries in the world, BRIC. She is fascinated by the way people are expressing themselves through digital social networks.

Elena Trost studied International Business with a specialisation in European Management at the Cologne Business School in Germany. In the scope of her studies, she followed her passion of travelling the world, learning about people's behaviour and experiencing new cultures. This allowed her to focus on psychology whilst studying in Montpellier, France and also culture and communications as part of her scholarship in Seoul, Korea.

Currently, she is working at Royal Philips Electronics Ltd. in the U.K. headquarters near London, responsible for different tasks in the field of social media marketing, operations and sales. Moreover, Elena is studying her Postgraduate degree in Strategic Marketing at the Oxford College of Marketing, where her current research includes emerging themes, corporate reputation and leadership.

Table of contents

I. Table of Contents

II. List of Figures

III. List of Tables

IV. List of Abbreviations

BMW	Bayrische Motorenwerke
BRIC	Brazil, Russia, India, China
CIS	Commonwealth of Independent States
E7	China, India, Brazil, Russia, Indonesia, Mexico, Turkey
G7	France, Germany, Italy, Japan, United Kingdom, United States, Canada
GDP	Gross Domestic Product
GNI	Gross National Income
PPP	Purchasing Power Parities
PwC	PricewaterhouseCoopers
SNS	Social Networking Sites
UGC	User-Generated Content

Preface

Based on the concepts of Milgram (1967), Granovetter (1973) and Burt (1992; 2004), this research highlights the potential of social media sites as tools for collective knowledge production and a viral spreading of information. Having identified social media sites as highly relevant instruments for corporate communications with customers in the context of social CRM, marketing, and R&D, Elena Trost inquires affordances of culturally adapted company presences in social network sites. This innovative study is of high interest as it studies the corporate use of social network sites targeting the emerging markets Brazil, Russia, India, and China -- so far a terrain largely inaccessible to English-speaking audiences.
I recommend this study to academic audiences and readers interested in practically integrating social media sites in social CRM, marketing, innovation management, and R&D approaches.

15 September 2013
Prof. Dr. Julia Maintz
Professor of International Management and Internet Economics, Cologne Business School

Acknowledgements

I would like to take the opportunity to thank several people for their support during the time of my research.

Special thank you goes out to my thesis advisor Prof. Dr. Julia Maintz, providing me with valuable insights and being available for all arising questions and difficulties with great enthusiasm.

Moreover, this book would not have been possible without the information gained from the user surveys and the expert interviews - thanks to Ruth Schöllhammer, Christian Offer, Alex Buchanan, Marc-Sven Kopka, Dr. Alexandra Wöllenstein and Jorge Junior.

Finally, I would like to thank my friends, especially Freddy, Susanne, Oliver and Burak, and my family, who supported me with new ideas and reinforcement during this period and helped me to start every day with new motivation.

Thank you!

Abstract

The economic growth and increasing Internet access within BRIC (Brazil, Russia, India and China) is opening new opportunities for companies to reach wider audiences.

This study examines these opportunities and assesses how global companies are capitalizing on these emerging markets; in particular the degree to which digital marketing and social CRM through social networks are being used. For the purposes of this analysis, three German brands are examined in detail: BMW, adidas and NIVEA.

The author shows that regular interaction with Internet users and monitoring of social networks can result in companies experiencing an uplift in both public perception and engagement. Another aspect addressed is the cultural variance that needs to be taken into account when planning social media activities. This study concludes that presently the full potential of social media has yet to be utilized within the BRIC countries, and that there is a unique opportunity to be realised by companies.

1 Introduction: An Overview of Digital Social Media in BRIC Countries

> We are in the midst of an accelerating, revolutionary transformation. Change is happening everywhere in technology, business, government, economics, organizational structures, values, and norms and consequently affects how we live, work and play (Toffler Associates 2012).

Today's companies face a world of global opportunities where the challenge lies in accessing them. An important focus in this context is the economic growth of the emerging markets as well as their technological advancement, including the increasing use of the Internet and social media tools. "Technology has made it possible for companies to expand into international markets. But doing so is complex" (Miller 2010: 2).

Being active in social media has become crucial for the vast majority of internationally operating companies, which intend to attract as many customers in the World Wide Web as possible with minimum efforts and costs. In his recent industry report "How marketers are using social media to grow their businesses", Stelzner (2010: 11-23) emphasises that a significant number (65%) of marketers have either just started to use social media or have been using it for only a few months. Moreover, at least 67% of marketers plan on increasing their use of blogs and various other social media networks. With regard to these facts, it can be said that companies are willing to expand their marketing strategies along with this trend. They are interested in communicating with an increasing number of people in less time (Mangold and Faulds 2009: 357). Nevertheless, when considering the aspect of entering digital social networks in different countries distinct cultural dimensions have to be understood and followed. Along with this trend of being active in social media, global companies are also keeping an eye on the rapid development of the emerging countries. Brazil, Russia, India and China, referred to as the 'BRIC' countries, belong to the fastest growing economies in the world and demonstrate an interesting target market for internationally operating companies.

> These countries account for more than a quarter of the world's land area and more than 40% of the world's population. They have changed their political systems to embrace global capitalism and are on track to be wealthier than most of today's economic powers by 2050 (Miller 2010: 2).

In order to connect a company's international marketing strategy to the social media networks of the BRIC countries, it seems inevitable to understand the dominating culture of the potential nation.

This book will focus on the following research question: Which success factors are crucial for companies when implementing social media marketing in the most relevant social networks of the BRIC countries? The link between the relevance of the virtual world and the core of the emerging markets will be shown with respect to the cases of BMW, adidas and NIVEA. The objective of this book is to emphasise the importance for globally operating companies to be present in digital social networks, such Facebook, VKontakte, Renren, and Kaixin001. Additionally, success factors of how companies implement their strategies in the best way will be demonstrated in the course of this research.

The paper starts with this introduction to the study focus: Social Media Marketing in BRIC countries: The case of BMW, adidas and NIVEA'.
In the beginning of the main part in chapter 2, the author will discuss the importance of social media. She will concentrate on the development of the World Wide Web, particularly the Web 2.0 and the trend of being active in social media. Subsequently, the author will discuss the relevance of social networks, one of the core elements of this paper. In this context, social media theories such as "Structural Holes" by Burt (Burt 1992; 2004), "The Small-World Problem" by Milgram (Milgram 1967) and "The Strength of Weak Ties" by Granovetter (Granovetter 1973) will be analysed. These theories will be applied specifically to digital social networks. Furthermore, social media marketing and its development will be outlined. As a last point, social media reception will be compared to usage trends of traditional media.
Chapter 3 (BRIC: Social Media beyond the "Big Four") will look at the increasing importance of the emerging markets. The spotlight will fall on BRIC, dynamic developing countries of the former third world (Goldman Sachs 2003: 11). After outlining the development, an outlook will demonstrate the continuing growth of the "Big Four". In order to link the topic of the BRIC countries to the virtual world, the importance of social media within these nations will be approached. In this context, the most relevant digital social networks of BRIC will provide deeper insights.
The following chapter 4 will outline the empirical approach. First, the companies BMW, adidas and NIVEA will be introduced briefly along with the motives for choosing them as case studies. Second, the author will describe the methodology, procedure of the investigation and the chosen qualitative and quantitative methods of the empirical research.
The discussion in chapter 5 (The Cases of BMW, adidas and NIVEA in SNS of the BRIC countries) will link the theory to the empirical investigation of the German brands BMW, adidas and NIVEA, and will evaluate the results of the quantitative and qualitative research. General survey results will serve as an introduction. Subsequently, the importance of social networks as important stimuli for innovation and the general presence of the three evaluated brands in social network sites of the BRIC countries will be examined. Then, social media marketing approaches will be set in relation to the findings. Finally, best practice suggestions will demonstrate possible ways to optimise social media presences of companies in social network sites of BRIC.
Chapter 6 (Conclusion: The Inevitability to Operate in Social Networks) summarises the most relevant findings of the research. Finally, in chapter 7, the author will outline future perspectives.
The following graph summarises the structure of this research to provide a general overview.

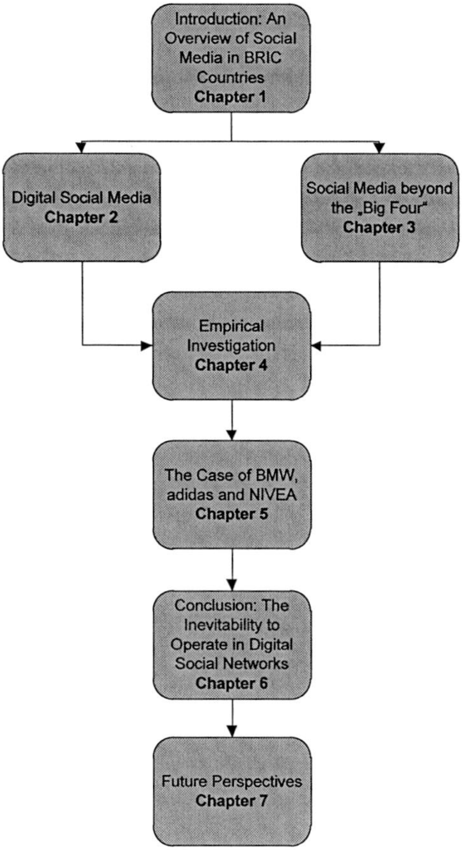

Figure 1: Structure of the Book
Source: Own Illustration.

2 Digital Social Media

"You cannot ignore this trend. You cannot sit this one out. [...] You may go a little slower or a little faster, but you have to move forward" (Li and Bernoff 2008: 75).

In recent years, digital social media reception rates have risen fast. The Internet, Web 2.0 and social media have promoted the transformation of our daily lives and profoundly contributed to societal change. Within this chapter, the concepts 'Internet', 'Web 2.0', 'social media' and 'social networks' will be explained. Subsequently, theories by Burt, Milgram and Granovetter are first outlined and then applied to digital social networks. Finally, social media marketing and its development are discussed and the shift towards "modern" forms of marketing in comparison to traditional marketing is highlighted.

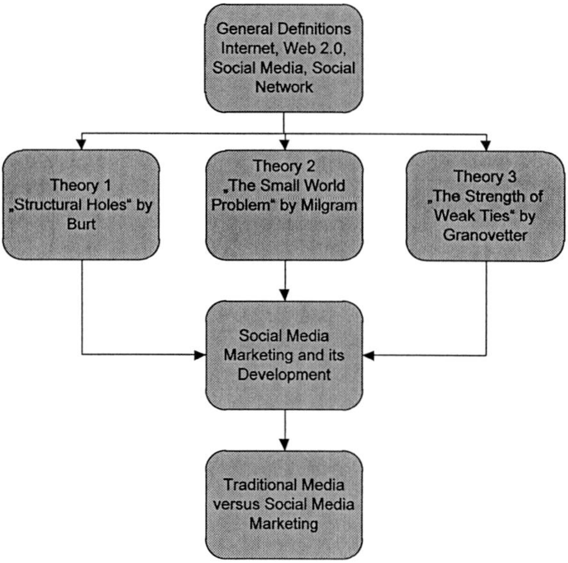

Figure 2: Structure of Chapter 2
Source: Own Illustration.

2.1 The Internet, Web 2.0, Social Media and Social Networks

The breakthrough of the Internet as a mass medium started with the establishment of the *World Wide Web* (www) delevoped by Tim Berners-Lee in 1989. The aim was to create a platform to save and share information which would be available to everyone (Hettler 2010: 1, 11). Different factors such as the development of new technologies, the improvement of data transmission, the reduction of Internet costs and the adaption of users' behaviour led to a widespread use of the Internet as a new tool for information exchange.

Web 2.0 is a term generally attributed to Tim O'Reilly, founder of the O'Reilly Media Group. According to Hettler (2010: 4), there is no generally accepted definition of Web 2.0, but different attempts have been made to describe it. In its broadest form, Web 2.0 is defined as an integration platform with the ability for users to create, modify and share information in an interconnected and 24 hour available virtual world.

> The advent of do-it-yourself publishing such as blogging and podcasting, coupled with social networking or socialcasting sites, such as MySpace and Facebook, created a new breed of content, known as User-Generated-Content (UGC) (Madia and Borgese 2010: 22).

O'Reilly (2006) describes Web 2.0 as

> the business revolution in the computer industry caused by the move to the Internet as platform, and an attempt to understand the rules for success on that new platform. Chief among those rules is this: build applications that harness network effects to get better the more people use them.

Social media is seen as a subset of Web 2.0, whereby users and user groups are increasingly becoming a major focus (Szugat, Gewehr & Lochmann 2006: 14; Hettler 2010: 14). Social media experts highlight that social media usage is characterized by content generation of people interested in representing themselves to the public. Social media serve as a virtual picture of real life where the contributions by people are totally free (Hettler 2010: 21; Interview III 2012: 2, 6). According to Bächle (2006: 121), social media usage is characterised the establishment and maintenance of social networks and virtual communities which are based on the principle of self-organisation. Additionally, these online platforms support the communication, interaction and cooperation between people.

Diverse online channels exist which provide platforms for users to create, upload, modify and share their contents:

> If we talk about social media in general, this is even more than just social networking. Social media is Wikipedia, Twitter, Blogs, YouTube, content sharing, slide sharing, forums and so on (Interview I 2012: 2).

All these tools and services share the common feature of encouraging social interaction (Hettler 2010: 41-64). In essence, the term social media includes all online platforms, applications and distribution channels, designed to integrate and engage target groups. This means that the interaction, sharing and collaboration centred on content between participants is facilitated (Madia and Borgese 2012: 12). The following picture (figure 3) shows the social media landscape and illustrates the various usage possibilities.

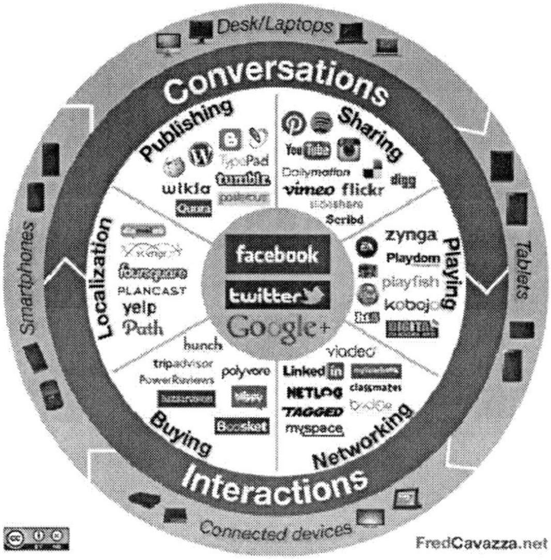

Figure 3: The Social Media Landscape 2012
Source: flickr fredcavazza 2008. Retrieved 11/04/2012, from http://www.flickr.com/photos/fredcavazza/2564571564/.

Within this paper, the author particularly focuses on the development of social networking sites (SNS). SNS are Web-based services which allow for information exchanges and communication between users and support the development and maintenance of relationships. Individuals can construct a public or semi-public profile within a bounded system, whereby they are able to articulate specific connections of their private or professional network. Moreover, their contact networks and those of other users active in the same social networking site can be traversed (Hettler 2010:54; Boyd and Ellison 2008: 211). What makes SNS unique is that they provide tools which allow users to share content and directly articulate and position themselves in the way they want to be perceived by others. By consisting of individual profiles which are designed and created by its members these social networks can be seen as an image of reality (Interview III 2012: 2, 6; Boyd and Ellison 2008: 210-211).

The reasons for people to join social networks are vast and varied. According to Madia and Borgese (2010: 24), the main reason of people's participation in social networking sites is that "people want a sense of belonging [...], the desire to satisfy the basic need of being a part of something". As soon as a humans' basic needs, such as food and shelter, belongings and esteem values like family and confidence, are satisfied, the desire of self-actualization comes into consideration (as conceptualised by Maslow in his hierarchy of needs: Maslow 1970:15-23). "Humans have an inniate need to be seen as important" (Madia and Borgese 2010: 25).

Through creation of the dialogue and direct engagement in social networks, this need is being fulfilled (Interview IV 2012: 2). In accordance with Mühlenbeck and Skibicki (2007: 43), not only is the need for communication an important reason to be a part of a SNS, but moreover the fun of participation and the establishment and maintenance of contacts are highly valued.

"When the mind is employed about a variety of objects it is somehow expanded and enlarged" (Smith 1964: 25). The analysis of social networks leads to mind-expanding theories such as *Structural Holes* by Burt, *The Small World Problem* by Milgram or *The Strength of Weak Ties* by Granovetter (Burt 1992; 2004; Milgram 1967; Granovetter 1973). In the course of the following three chapters, these approaches will be outlined in more detail and put in relation to digital social networks.

2.2 Structural Holes

Network structures connected by bridges can be found in a wide variety of contexts. Whether in communities in a geographic area or divisions in a corporation, people form network structures which may be clustered and may integrate via bridges across these network constellations. Within one group, people's ways of thinking and behaving tends to be more homogenous than between groups. Individuals or groups representing alternative ways of thinking and behaving can connect, if different network segments or clusters are bridged. Since these interconnections enable more options to synthesise and to select from, new ideas are emerging across the structural holes between groups (Burt 2004: 349-352).

Within his studies "Structural holes and good ideas" and "Structural holes, the social structure of competition", Ronald Burt outlines the social structure of networks in connection to the existence of so-called "structural holes" (Burt 1992; 2004). According to Burt, the number of non-redundant contacts constitutes an important aspect in social networks. He argues that contacts are redundant in a network, if the same people are active and therefore the same information circulates. Burt further describes the separation between non-redundant contacts as a structural hole, "the relationship of non-redundancy between two contacts" (Burt 1992: 18). The hole between the contacts serves as a buffer or insulator and consequently the two contacts provide network benefits which are "in some degree additive rather than overlapping" (Burt 1992: 18). The creation of groups and structural holes is illustrated in figure 4.

The structure of different networks represented in illustration (figure 4) corresponds to Émile Durkheim's "division du travail social" (Durkheim 1893: 3-10). Different networks and relationships are illustrated in the picture. Structural holes separate non-redundant contacts. Bridges over these structural holes lead to important connections which then link separate networks and connect different information pools. Since it can be expected that the number of structural holes increases with network size and the holes represent the keys to information benefits, especially large social networks refer to opportunities to recombine information, i.e. the promotion of learning and innovation by a combination of these information reservoirs (Burt 1992: 20).

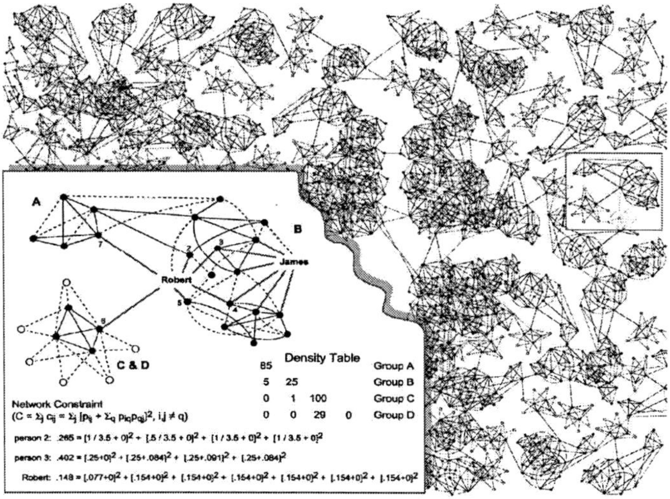

Figure 4: The Small World of Markets and Organizations
Source: Burt 2004: 352.

2.3 The Small-World Problem

"The simplest way of formulating the small-world problem is: Starting with any two people in the world, what is the probability that they will know each other?" (Milgram 1967: 62).

The concept of "six degrees of separation" originated from Stanley Milgram's "Experimental study of the small-world problem" where he outlines that any two people in the world can be linked in terms of intermediate acquaintances (Milgram 1967). The number of those intermediate links will be relatively small. In his experiment, Milgram asked people in city A to generate acquaintance chains to a target person in city B. His results demonstrated that for those who reached the target person the mean number of intermediaries was 5.2 between starter and target (Milgram 1967: 63; Travers and Milgram 1969: 425). This phenomenon is illustrated the following graph (figure 5).
In accordance with Milgram (1969: 425-426), people might share one or more mutual acquaintances without knowing each other directly. Within this set of individuals, person A and person Z may not only be connected by any single common acquaintance, but through a series of intermediaries. Therefore, the structure of connections between people takes the form of a cluster composed of a complex web of connections.

> The phrase "small-world" suggests that social networks are in a sense tightly woven and full of unexpected strands linking individuals who are seemingly far removed from one another in physical or social space (Milgram 1969: 426).

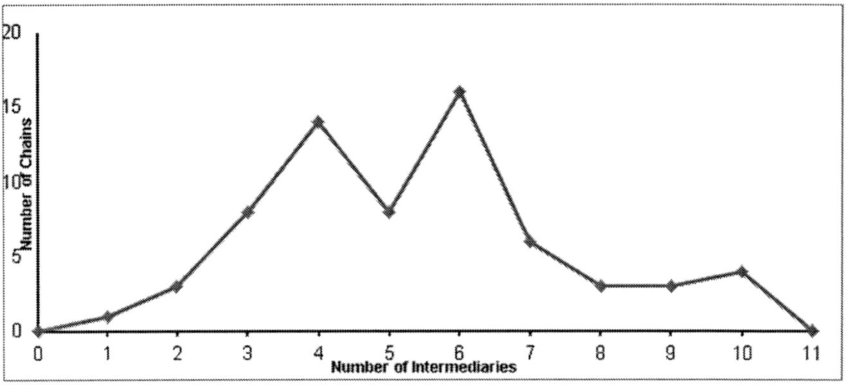

Figure 5: Lengths of Completed Chains
Source: Reproduction of Milgram 1969: 433.

2.4 The Strength of Weak Ties

Relationships are critical concerning the creation of knowledge and its transfer. The structural benefit of weak ties is the access to non-redundant information (Levin and Cross 2004: 1477). In "The strength of weak ties", Granovetter defines the "strength" of an interpersonal tie in the following way:

> The strength of a tie is a (probably linear) combination of the amount of time, the emotional intensity, the intimacy (mutual confiding), and the reciprocal services which characterise the tie. Each of these is somewhat independent of the other, though the set is obviously highly intercorrelated (Granovetter 1973: 1362).

Concerning the micro level, Granovetter suggests the following basic model of a relationship between the node points A, B and C.

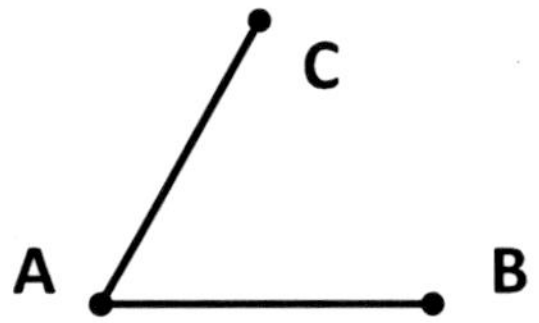

Figure 6: A Basic Model of Relationship
Source: Reproduction of Granovetter 1973: 1363.

The occurrence of a relationship or tie between the node points B and C is likely, if the node points A and B as well as A and C are strongly linked. Moreover, along with the intensity of a relationship, the number of shared friends increases which emphasises the significance of "bridges" within a network. These bridges are defined as "lines in a network, which provide the only path between two points". Granovetter concludes that no strong tie is a bridge and therefore "all bridges are weak ties" (Granovetter 1973: 1363, 1364). Weak ties are more likely to link members of different groups in networks than strong ones. Weak ties connect different actors and consequently enable the flow of information (figure 7).

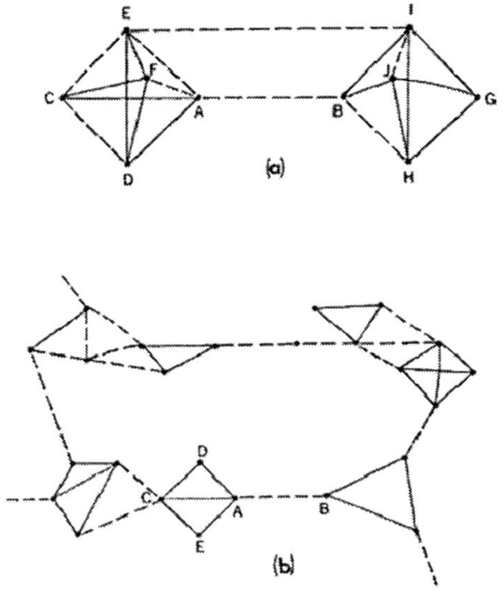

Figure 7: Network Connection through Strong and Weak Ties
Source: Granovetter 1973: 1365.

Information passing through weak ties can "reach a larger number of people" and "traverse greater social distance" (Granovetter 1973: 1366).

2.5 The Development of Social Media Marketing

> Marketing is a process of planning and executing: The conception, pricing, promotion, and the distribution of goods and services to facilitate exchanges that satisfy individuals and organizational objectives (Nickels, McHugh & McHugh 2008: 350).

The term 'marketing' is used in a variety of contexts: Individuals and organizations can hereby satisfy their needs through the creation and the exchange of values with others. In social and managerial processes, marketing involves building profitable and value-laden relationships with customers. Companies create values for their clients and try to establish strong customer relationships with the aim of capturing value from them in return.

Moreover, marketing can also be seen as a social technique to implement ideas with a societal benefit (Armstrong et al. 2009: 7; Meffert, Burmann & Kirchgeorg 2008: 3; Hettler 2010: 37). It becomes more and more important to consider how the perspective of the customer on the one hand and the perspective of performance on the other hand can be managed. The aim of marketing continously adapted to new requirements since the 1950s (comp. figure 8).

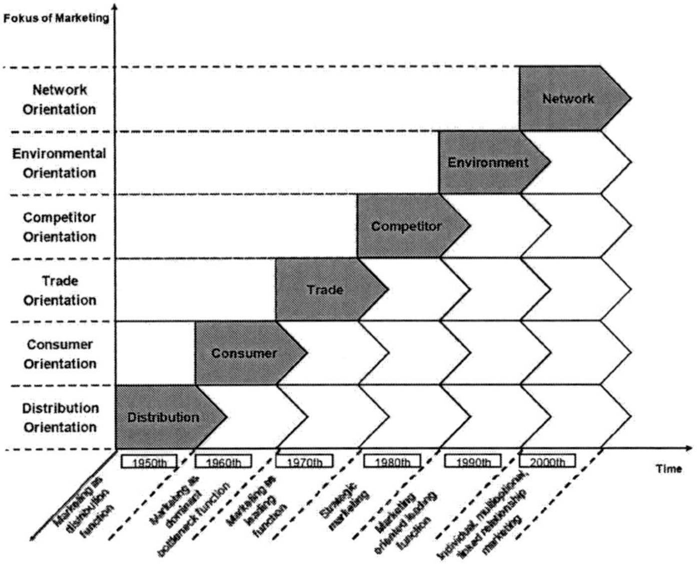

Figure 8: Levels of Marketing Development
Source: Meffert, Burmann & Kirchgeorg 2008: 8.

Social media marketing focuses on the question which instruments are needed, in order to attract the customer's attention: marketing with the target-oriented use of social media. New possibilities and opportunities of the World Wide Web to publish user-generated content and to directly engage with customers are given priority. Social media marketing involves customers in communication processes through diverse Web 2.0 applications. Users of social media platforms provide valuable content, such as suggestions regarding product or service improvements, innovative product ideas and information about product preferences. This online engagement and the creation of content serve as a method to achieve the marketing objectives. Social media has become a hybrid element of the promotion mix. User engagement however needs time and effort, in order to be realised. Social media marketing focuses on attracting people, delighting and inspiring them to get involved in marketing and brand promotion processes.

Attempts are being made to generate emotional incentives, in order to trigger an intended action, such as the recommendation of a brand or product-related suggestions. This information can also be integrated in approaches to further develop the product. In the context of this research, social media marketing is seen as a method to influence the target group, in order to reach desired actions like product-related transactions, recommendations or suggestions.

The maxime should be the direct engagement and dialogue with customers through the use of social media (Hettler 2010: 37-39; Mangold and Faulds 2009: 357).

> The content, timing, and frequency of the social media-based conversations occurring between consumers are outside managers' direct control. This concept stands in contrast to the traditional integrated marketing communications paradigm, where a high degree of control is present (Mangold and Faulds 2009: 357).

Traditional media, such as print, radio or TV, are reaching fewer and fewer people. The tendency to shift marketing budgets to the Internet has already been proven by several studies (absatzwirtschaft 2008; Hettler 2012: 30). The increased interest in social media marketing is also illustrated by the increase of the use of the term 'social media marketing' in general (figure 9). Moreover, it is expressed in statistics concerning the development of the social media budgets in companies (figure 10).

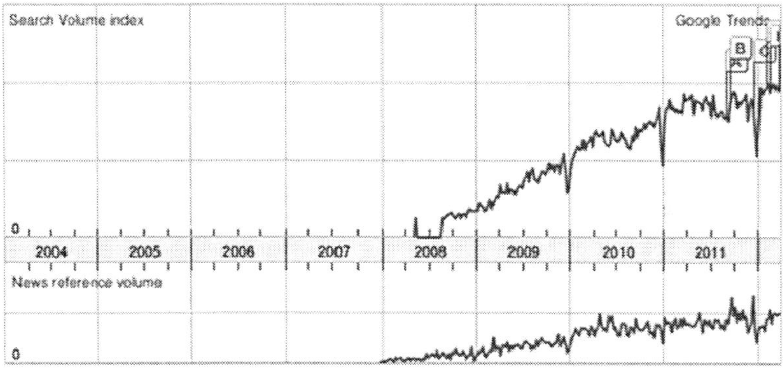

Figure 9: Development of the Word "Social Media Marketing"
Source: Google trends 2012. Retrieved 02/04/2012 from
http://www.google.de/trends/?q=social+media+marketing.

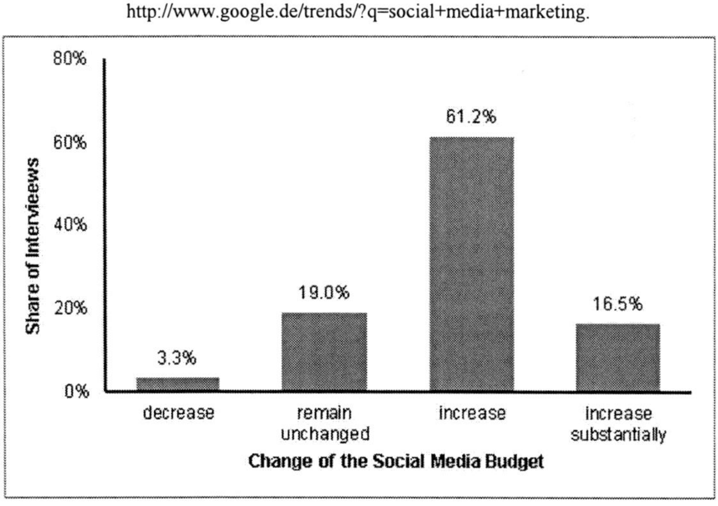

Figure 10: Change of Social Media Budgets in Companies
Source: Reproduction of BVDW 2007. Retrieved 04/04/2012 from Statista database.

Figure 10 indicates that more than 75% of respondents of a BVDW study (2007: 1) asked about the development of the social media expenditures of their companies were of the opinion that they would at least increase. Twenty percent of these respondents stated that they would even rise sharply. There are differences between social media marketing and 'traditional' marketing approaches. The next chapter gives detailed insights about this distinction.

2.6 Traditional Media vs. Social Media Marketing

One of the best approaches to reach most companies' target groups is a Web-based procedure. Social media tools provide interaction and involvement opportunities, which offers the possibility to enter into direct contact with the target audience: "Involvement heißt das Zauberwort im World Wide Web" (Schwarz 2008: 20). Compared to other traditional forms of media such as TV, radio or newspapers,

> social media's claim to fame is that it is customizable, portable, time-shifted and endlessly shareable, offering a constant connection to concentric circles of online communities (Madia and Borgese 2010: 12).

The enhanced one-to-one, one-to-many and many-to-many dialogues which can be established through social media constitute a major difference to traditional media. With the growing importance of the Internet, the balance is shifting from traditional mass media towards diverse forms of online communication. This tendency can be recognised in the following result (figure 11) of a survey by Zerfass et al. (2011). Over 2,000 public relations professionals answered the following question: How important are the following methods in addressing stakeholders, gatekeepers and audiences? Will this change within the next three years? (Hettler 2010: 31; Interview V 2012: 4-5).

2011		In 2014		
1	Press and media relations: Print media	1	Online communication	↗
2	Online communication	2	Press and media relations: Online media	↗
3	Press and media relations: Online media	3	Social media	↑
4	Face-to-face communication	4	Face-to-face communication	→
5	Press and media relations: TV/radio	5	Press and media relations: Print media	↓

Figure 11: Change in Communication Modes
Source: Reproduction of Zerfass et al. 2011. Retrieved 11/04/2012, from http://www.zerfass.de/ecm/ECM2011-Results-ChartVersion.pdf.

The shift from print to online communication, including an increasing use of social media, implies that companies have to adapt their marketing strategies to the new requirements of their customers.

In accordance with the marketing expert Wöllenstein (Interview V 2012: 7-9), being present where your customers are and modifying your strategy with regard to your target group is one of the most crucial aspects companies have to face nowadays. This adaption is already in process as companies are increasing their expenditures for online advertisement on a regular basis. Within a time span of eight years (2008-2016), these expenditures are expected to more than double, as shown in figure 12. The reference research was conducted between 2000 and 2009. The years from 2009 to 2016 are based on a projection (Magnaglobal 2011: 1).

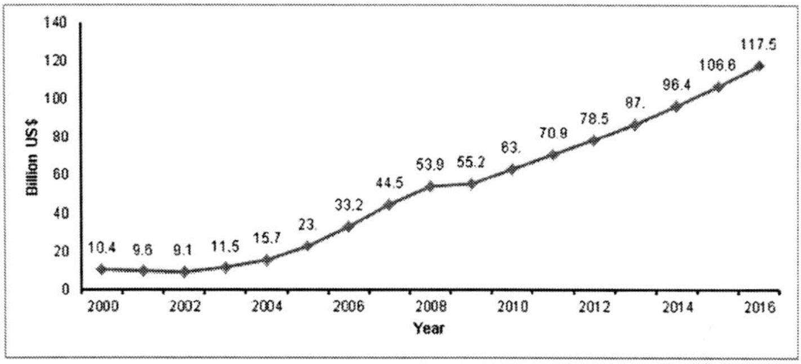

Figure 12: Expenditures for Online Advertisement Worldwide in bn. US $
Source: Reproduction of Magnaglobal 2011. Retrieved 03/04/2012, from http://de.statista.com/statistik/daten/studie/185637/umfrage/Prognose-der-Entwicklung-der-Ausgaben-für-Online-Werbung-weltweit/.

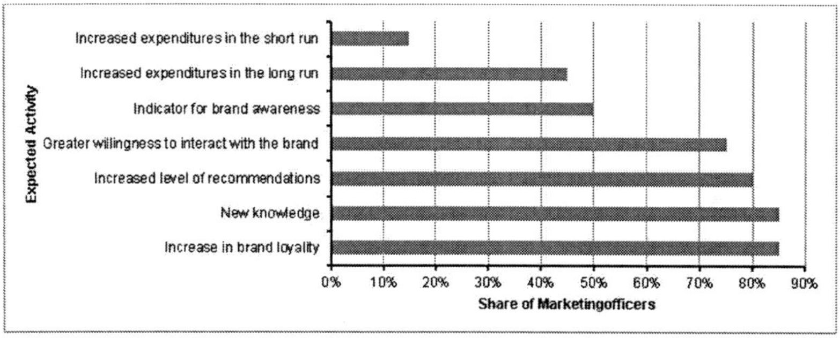

Figure 13: Expectations of Companies' Activity in the Social Web
Source: Reproduction of Millward Brown Optimor (2011). Retrieved 03/04/2012, from Statista database: http://de.statista.com/statistik/daten/studie/184753/umfrage/erwartungen-von-unternehmen-im-social-web/.

New expectations by companies arise with the move towards online advertisement. According to a survey of Optimor (2011), 85% of the responsible marketing managers expect to gain new knowledge about their products and customers by using the Internet. A greater willingness to interact with the firms as well as an increased level of recommendations within the social Web could imply higher expenditures for firms in the long term which is expected by nearly half of the participants.

More than 80% of the marketing managers anticipate an increase in brand loyality within the respective company, which is illustrated in the following bar chart (figure 13).
The vast majority of companies faces challenges when adapting to social media marketing. Through digital mouth-to-mouth propaganda via the Internet, such as posting contents in social networks, contributions often stay present in the digital world and can still be found after years. Since social media channels foster this digital mouth-to-mouth propaganda enormously, they help to distribute information within a community. As shown in an online global consumer study by Nielsen (2007), people trust recommendations from consumers to an extent of 78%. The confidence of different forms of advertisement was examined. In social media, especially in social networks, where the direct contact between participants is enabled, the word-of-mouth logic is a crucial point for companies to be kept in mind. Influencing word-of-mouth contents is the core of viral marketing. The aim to reach a specific marketing objective within a given time frame is part of social media marketing (Hettler 2010: 77-78).
How to adapt in the best way depends on several factors. "Wer glaubt, dass allein durch die Präsenz im Internet die Bekanntheit eines Unternehmens gesteigert wird, der träumt" (Schwarz 2008: 43). It is not enough just to be present in SNS as companies must always invest resources, especially time and effort. They should not expect the marketing approach to run automatically. "Das ist ein Trugschluss" (Interview IV 2012: 8). "Das ist ungefähr so, als ob Sie mitten in der Sahara einen Getränkestand aufbauen. Die Idee ist gut, aber reich werden Sie damit nicht, weil keine Kunden kommen" (Schwarz 2008: 43).
One of the first questions companies should ask themselves is what they are expecting to achieve with their social media marketing activities and how they intend to achieve it. Whether the company is interested in improving the image of the company, boosting its product information or developing customer loyalty, the strategy has to be adapted and different methods have to be applied. In social media it is now possible to directly communicate with customers and to learn from them in the form of a dialogue. This can be measured through different criteria such as 'likes', which means approvals by users, numbers of fans or qualitative analysis of customers' engagement (Schwarz 2008: 216; Interview I 2012: 5-9).
Considering the diverse aspects mentioned above, social media marketing is currently developing into one of the most important marketing tools used by an increasing number of companies. As a result, new challenges have to be faced, problems tackled and strategies adapted. Companies are approaching a new digital development which can lead to growth when applied in the right way.
As social media is increasing on a continuous basis throughout the world, globally operating companies should consider the latest virtual trends in the target market. The BRIC countries represent major present and future economies. More and more investors are observing BRIC markets, also in terms of social networks, in order to increase their brands popularity and learn directly from their customers. The next chapter will highlight insights about the emerging markets and SNS in BRIC countries.

3 BRIC – Social Media beyond "the Big Four"

> A stumble or two will not change the longer-term global power shift, from ex-Christendom to the world symbolized by the BRICs. So far, the economies concerned have been almost as solid as, well, a brick (Swann and Hadas 2011).

This chapter is concerned with the general development of emerging markets followed by a future outlook. Social media marketing in the BRIC countries will be examined in more detail. Furthermore, the SNS of these important markets are explained, in order to be closer examined in the empirical investigation of BMW, adidas and NIVEA's presence in these SNS (chapter 4).

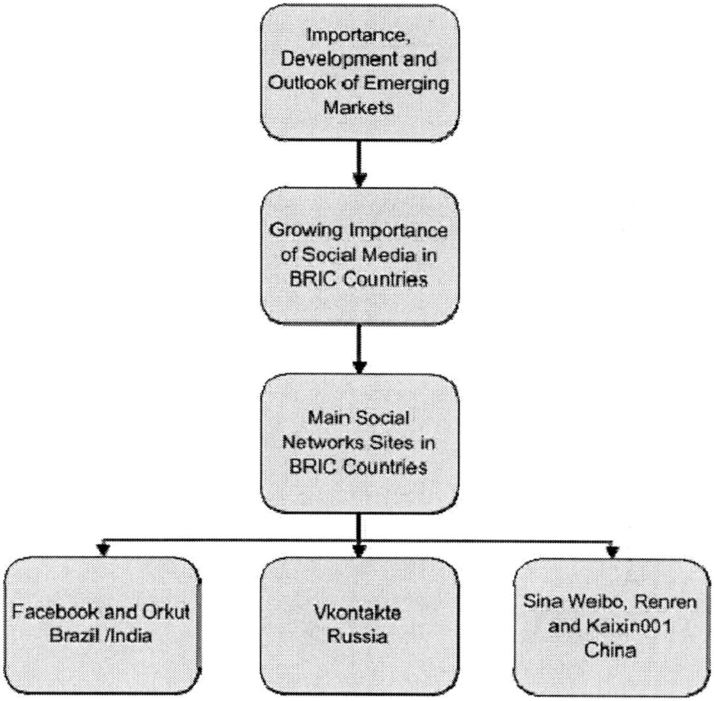

Figure 14: Structure of Chapter 3
Source: Own Illustration.

3.1 The Development of Emerging Markets

As pioneer who coined the term 'emerging markets', World Bank economist Antoine van Agtmael (2007: 384) states that "the world's center of gravity is already tipping decisively in favor of the emerging economies". The emerging markets can be split into four regions, Asia, Emerging Europe, Latin America and the so called "frontier" markets, broadly to be found in Africa and the Middle East. Within the development of these areas, all regions have certain attractions and carry general risk. They provide a wide range of opportunities, exhibit high expected returns as well as high volatility (Marr and Reynard 2010: 3; Harvey 1994: 2).
At their broadest over 140 countries are defined as emerging markets. They represent about 84% of the world's population and almost 75% of the world's land surface. Relative to mature markets, the expenditures in worldwide technology are steadily increasing in these growing economies. Moreover, emerging markets account for about 70% of global exchange reserves and for more than 50% of the global energy consumption. According to some prognoses, in terms of the combined Gross Domestic Products (GDP) the top 20 developed economies will be surpassed by the emerging market nations by 2015. In the following illustration, it is distinguished between three subgroups of emerging markets according to market size (population) and economic attractiveness (GNI per capita): long-term opportunity markets, niche opportunity markets and strategic opportunity markets are outlined in figure 15 (Marr and Reynard 2010: 3; Vital Wave Consulting 2009: 1-4).

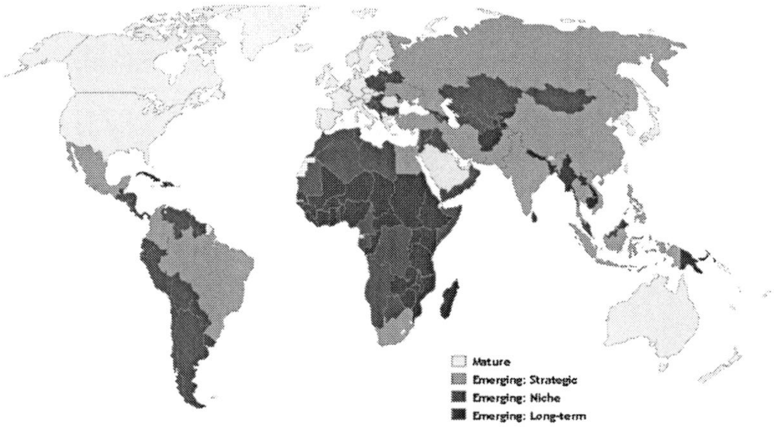

Figure 15: Overview of Emerging Markets
Source: Vital Wave Consulting 2009: 1, based on World Bank data. Retrieved 05/04/2012, from http://www.vitalwaveconsulting.com/pdf/Emerging%20Markets%20Definition%20and%20World%20Market%20Groups.pdf.

The strategic opportunity markets (figure 15) with a population over 40 million and a strong GDP growth, represent the largest and most attractive economies for multinational corporations, trying to enlarge their customer base. These markets include the BRIC countries, which will in the context of this study be focused on in more detail.
The term BRIC the author introduced in chapter 2, refers to the countries Brazil, Russia, India and China and was coined by Jim O'Neill, chairman of Goldman Sachs, in his paper "Building Better Global Economic BRICs" of 2001. Also known as "The Big Four", the BRIC countries represent the fastest growing economies in the world and therefore interesting target markets for globally operating companies.

> These countries account for more than a quarter of the world's land area and more than 40 percent of the world's population. They have changed their political systems to embrace global capitalism and are on track to be wealthier than most of today's economic powers by 2050 (Miller 2010: 2).

Based on figures of the United Nations, figure 16 demonstrates that the population of the BRIC countries has more than doubled in the past 50 years, representing around three billion people today.

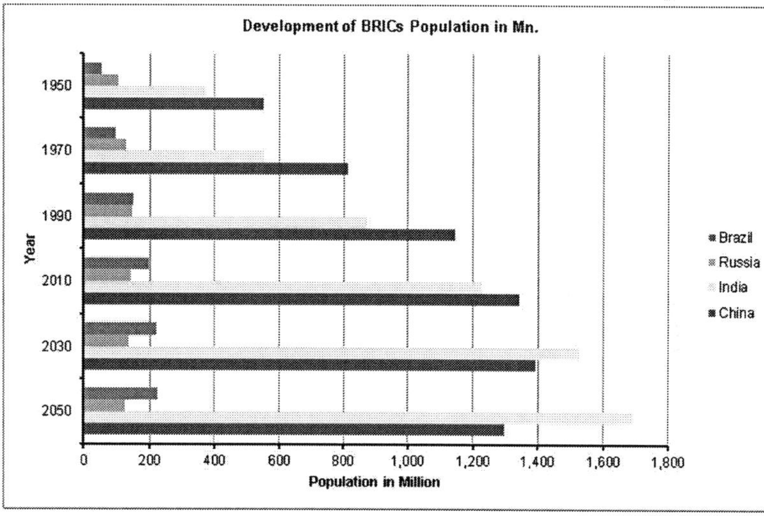

Figure 16: Population Growth in BRIC Countries
Source: Reproduction of United Nations (2010). Retrieved 21/04/2012, from http://esa.un.org/unpd/wpp/index.htm.

Moreover, the GDP of the enormous population is an important aspect in terms of economic growth of BRIC. According to some predictions of Goldman Sachs (2003: 4), the BRICs' aggregate GDP could account for over half the size of the G6's GDP by 2040 in US $ (figure 17).

The abbreviation G6 here refers to France, Germany, Italy, Japan, The United Kingdom and the United States.

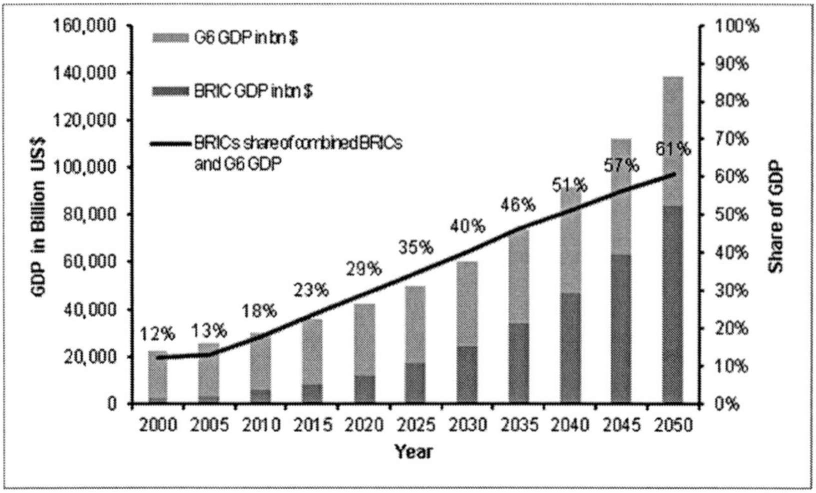

Figure 17: BRICs Share of GDP
Source: Reproduction of Goldman Sachs 2003: 4. Retrieved 06/04/2012, from http://www.goldmansachs.com/our-thinking/brics/brics-reports-pdfs/brics-dream.pdf.

This enormous GDP growth does not only contribute to an increase in wealth of the BRIC countries, but is as well a reason why many foreign investors are operating here. Concerning foreign imports and direct investment, in 2009, for the first time, more than half of all foreign investments went to emerging markets. This also emphasises the key relevance of these new economic areas, forcing globally operating companies to develop new internationalisation strategies. In the upcoming chapter, a further outlook of the BRIC countries is given and provides insights on expected future developments (Meckl 2010: 319; Kekic 2009: 4).

3.2 Outlook

By 2050, the BRIC countries, as the fastest growing economies in the world, will have overtaken most of today's economic powers (Miller 2010: 2). In "Dreaming With BRICs", Goldman Sachs (2003: 1-24) outlined several predictions about the developing paths to 2050. In connection to the study of PwC (2011: 1-25), challenges and opportunities for "The Big Four" will be outlined in the course of this chapter.

Accelerated by the recent global financial crisis, a rapid convergence between the E7 (China, India, Brazil, Russia, Indonesia, Mexico and Turkey), the world's largest emerging economies and the G7 (G6 and Canada), the world largest economies in general, can be recognised.

This can be seen in figure 18, outlining the shrinking gap and final overtaking of the G7 by the E7 in terms of GDP at PPP (Purchasing Power Parities). GDP at PPP is an indicator of the average living standard, since it corrects price differences across countries at different levels of development.

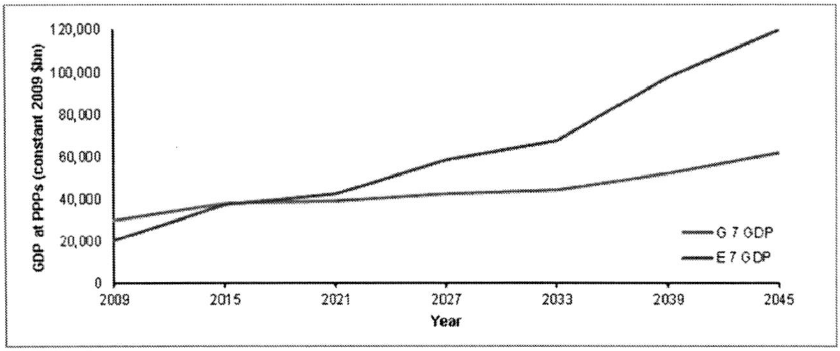

Figure 18: G7 and E7 – GDP at PPPs Projections
Source: Reproduction of PwC 2011: 8.

The graph demonstrates that the catch-up process is expected to continue until 2020. By then, GDP at PPP of E7 could already be higher than total G7 GDP at PPP. The process of overtaking in the following decades is likely to be reinforced by the E7, it's expected to be almost twice as large as the G7 GDP at PPP in 2050. According to PwC (2011: 8), China and India represent the key drivers of the E7.
Despite an overall slowdown of the growth within the BRIC countries, China is expected to overtake the US as the world's largest economy, measured by GDP (figure 19). By 2050, China is expected to take the first place, India the third, Brazil the fifth and Russia the sixth place.

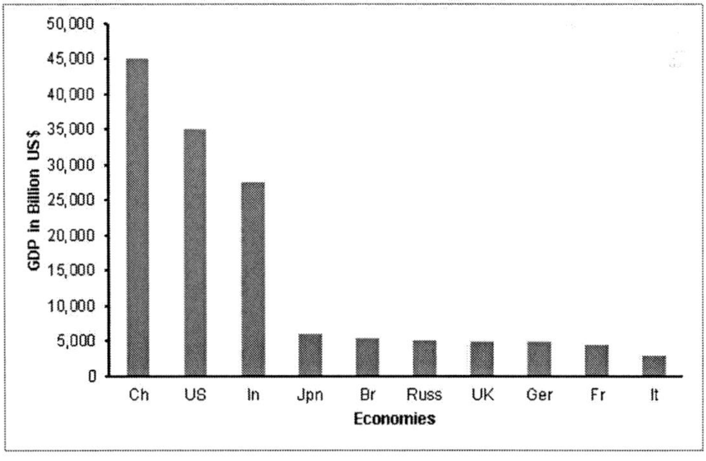

Figure 19: The World's Largest Economies in 2050
Source: Reproduction of Goldman Sachs 2003: 4.

The graph demonstrates that the BRIC countries are going to belong to the leaders of the world's largest markets.
Additionally, taking into consideration the annual increase in US dollar spending from the BRIC countries, by 2025 the increase could be twice of the G6's US dollar spending increase and by 2050 even four times higher (figure 20). Moreover, forecasts predict that within 50 years, the consolidated GDP per capita of Brasil, Russia, India and China will grow by nearly 1,200%. Whereas in the year 2000, the GDP per capita in total for BRIC was about $10,000, it is likely to increase to $130,000 in 2050 (figure 21).

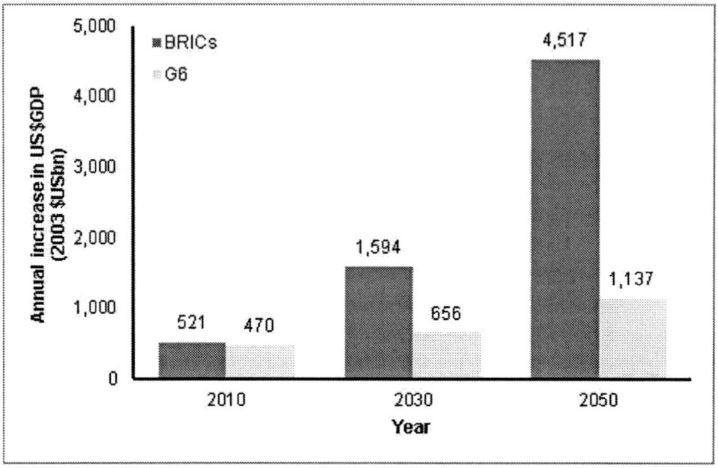

Figure 20: Difference in Demand: BRIC vs. G6
Source: Reproduction of Goldman Sachs 2003: 5.

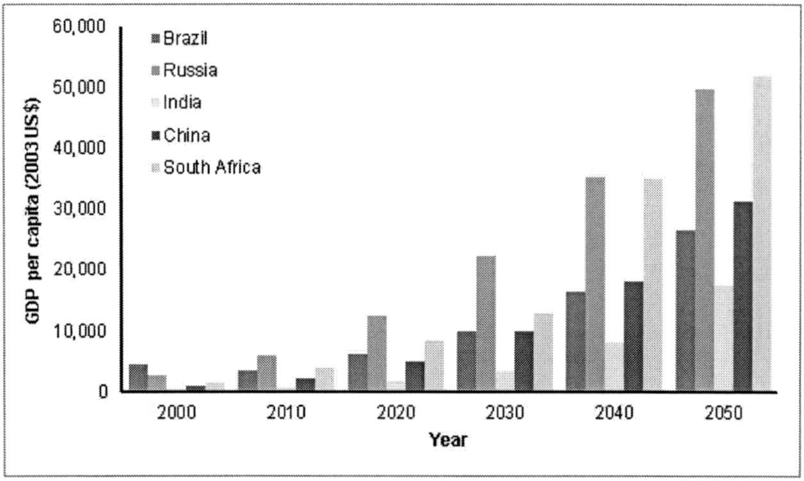

Figure 21: GDP per Capita in BRIC
Source: Reproduction of Goldman Sachs 2003: 11.

Overall, it can be concluded that BRIC countries continue to be interesting markets with valuable investment prospects - it is assumed that these countries are becoming a much stronger force in the world economy. Diverse challenges arise from the rapid growth of the emerging markets. Just to mention two examples, the pressure on natural resources as well as implications for climate change have to be faced (PwC 2011: 24-25; Borodina and Shvyrkov 2010: xiv).

> The relative importance of the BRICs as an engine of new demand growth and spending power may shift more dramatically and quickly than expected. Higher growth in these economies could offset the impact of greying populations and slower growth in the advanced economies (Goldman Sachs 2003: 2).

The economic growth of BRIC economies is also reflected in increasing social media activities in these markets, which is discussed in the following chapter.

3.3 The Growing Importance of Social Media in BRIC Countries

The growth of social media is going to have large impact on the daily life of nearly every one of us.

> In the future, we will no longer search for products and services; rather they will find us via social media. Businesses don't have the choice on whether or not they do social media, the choice is on how well they do it (Qualman 2011: xxi).

Since social media is a topic affecting not only particular nations, also the BRIC countries are floating with the present. Within this chapter, the growing importance of social media in these emerging markets will be highlighted. After giving a short introduction, the main SNS are going to provide more detailed insights of the BRIC's virtual worlds.

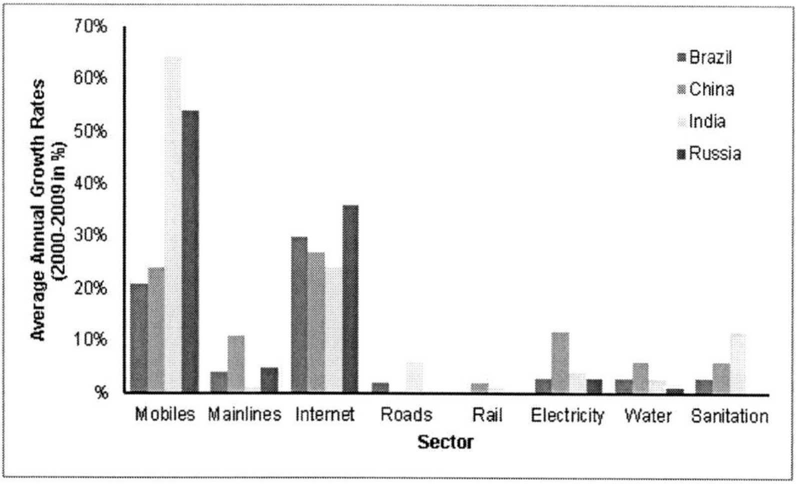

Figure 22: Infrastructure in BRIC Countries
Source: Reproduction of Goldman Sachs 2011: 1.

In recent years, technical infrastructure has improved notably in the BRIC countries. In particular cell phone distribution and Internet connectivity have developed rapidly (figure 22; Goldman Sachs 2011: 1).
Concerning advertisement marketing, the biggest winners of market volume will be China, Russia and Brazil. By 2013, China is expected to overtake Germany and become the third largest ad market. Brazil is stated to become number six, while Russia is expected to rise from the twelfth place to number ten. While TV will reign supremely for the foreseeable future, online advertisement is expected to rise constantly. It is predicted that by 2013 digital advertisement will have become the second biggest medium and overtake newspaper advertisement (Parekh 2011: 1). These changes are demonstrated in table 1, comparing the ten top advertisement markets in 2010 and 2013.

Rank	**2010**	**2013 (forecast)**
1	USA	USA
2	Japan	Japan
3	Germany	**China**
4	**China**	Germany
5	UK	UK
6	France	**Brazil**
7	**Brazil**	**Russia**
8	Italy	France
9	Australia	Italy
10	Canada	Australia

Table 1: Top 10 Ad Markets in 2010 and 2013
Source: Reproduction of Parekh 2011: 1. Retrieved 07/04/2012, from http://adage.com/article/mediaworks/global-ad-spending-grow-4-2/226903/.

It is assumed in the course of this study that access to telecommunications in BRIC is going to increase further. Adapting to and being active in some of the world's most promising markets seems to be one of the biggest challenges for globally operating companies such as BMW, adidas and NIVEA (chapter 5). In the following chapter, the most relevant SNS of BRIC will be presented.

3.4 The Main Social Network Sites in BRIC Countries

Defining social networks at the most basic level, they correspond to Internet communities in which individuals interact and present themselves and their networks through self-generated profiles. SNS offer a new dimension of people's lives. Everyone is able to share information he or she wants and to engage in specific topics or discussions (Interview III 2012: 2; Interview II 2012: 2).
Nobody is literally forced to join these online networks, but rather encouraged to use them and reveal personal information. This engagement is furthermore simplified by easy access and tools which allow for an uncomplicated sharing of information. At the same time, the costs of Internet usage und data store continue to decline. The majority of SNS are for free, excluding extra functions, which attracts even more users. These aspects imply that people with the need to share information increasingly use SNS. Around the world, diverse online SNS have experienced exponential growth of memberships in recent years and cannot be seen as a niche phenomenon anymore (Acquisti and Gross 2006: 36-38; Hettler 2010: 6). Within different cultures, several preferences can also be recognized in terms of the use of various digital social networks. In the context of this study, the following social network sites of each BRIC country will be examined (table 2). Companies such as BMW, adidas and NIVEA, which have been chosen as examples in this study, are using these SNS to optimise their marketing approaches (chapter 5).

Social Network	**Country**
Facebook, Orkut	Brazil, India
VKontakte	Russia
Sina Weibo, Renren, Kaixin001	China

Table 2: SNS in BRIC
Source: Own Illustration.

3.4.1 Facebook and Orkut

In Brazil and India, Facebook has overtaken the use of Google's SNS Orkut. Launched in 2004, Facebook became very popular in both countries during the last decade. Referring to statistics of Ibope Nielsen Online, Forbes (2011: 1) outlines that in terms of users, the "Facebook revolution" occurred and lead to a shift away from the SNS Orkut. The following graphic also demonstrates the increasing use of Facebook (Google trends, figure 23). At this point, more detailed information about Orkut is set aside and in the context of this research, it will be focused more on the largest and most relevant SNS in BRIC countries, which are of high interest to global companies.
The relevance of Facebook in Brazil as well as India is further highlighted (see the statistics of Socialbakers 2012, table 3). The top ten countries in terms of user populations of the first quarter of 2012 on Facebook are represented, placing India on the second and Brazil on the third place.

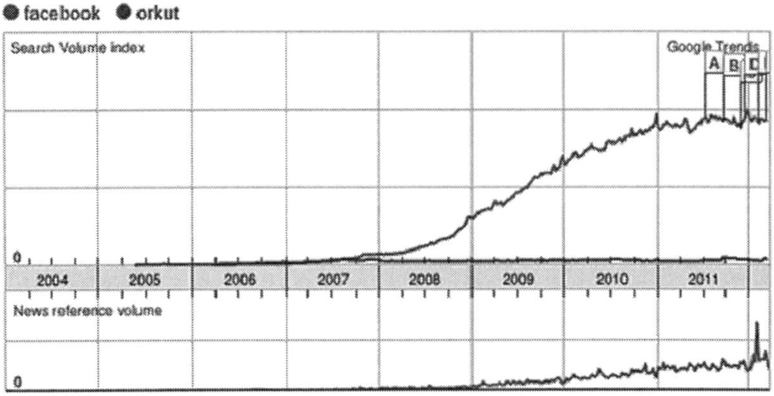

Figure 23: Facebook vs. Orkut in Google Trends
Source: Google trends. Retrieved 01/04/2012, from http://www.google.de/trends/?q=Facebook,+Orkut.

#	Country	User	Change
1	United States	+ 5,400,220	+ 3.57%
2	India	+ 8,418,860	+22.52%
3	Brazil	+ 15,320,200	+52.28%
4	Indonesia	+ 2,169,660	+5.36%
5	Mexico	+ 3,285,020	+11.02%
6	Turkey	+ 355,020	+1.16%
7	United Kingdom	+ 144880	+0.48%
8	Philippines	+ 459,920	+ 27.36%
9	France	+ 954, 380	+ 37.28%
10	Germany	+ 1,947,840	+28.45%

Table 3: Countries on Facebook
Source: Reproduction of Socialbakers 2012. Retrieved 12/04/2012, from http://www.socialbakers.com/facebook-statistics/?interval=last-6-months#chart-intervals.

Facebook, launched by a computer science student in 2004 at Harvard University, developed high coverage around the world (figure 24). Mark Zuckerberg, CEO and founder of Facebook, states that the mission of this SNS would be to make the world more open and connected. Available in more than 70 languages, this SNS should help people to stay in touch with friends and family and to discover recent news and trends all over the world. Moreover, people are enabled to share and express their opinions. In the beginning of the year 2012, Facebook claimed to have about 845 million monthly active users and nearly 500 million daily active users on average (figures 25 and 26). In accordance with Internet World Stats (2011), more than 30% of the world's population is using the Internet. Of these 2.3 billion Internet users in the world, around 900 million are registered on Facebook, representing 40% of the whole Internet population.

According to Qualman (2011: xxii), "if Facebook was a country, it would be the third largest country in the world behind only China and India". Keeping in mind the increasing trend of more and more people registering every day, it is likely that Facebook will keep its position as the most relevant SNS of the world (Madia and Borgese 2010: 99; Facebook 2012: 1-3; eBiz MBA 2012).

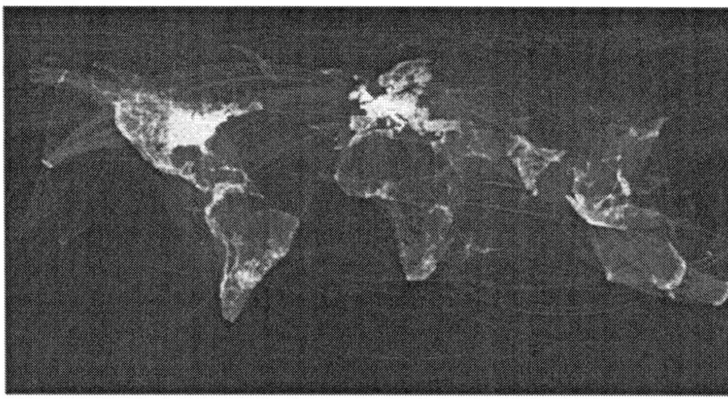

Figure 24: Facebook's World Activity
Source: United States Securities and Exchange Commission (2011). Retrieved 09/04/2012, from http://sec.gov/Archives/edgar/data/1326801/000119312512034517/d287954ds1.htm.

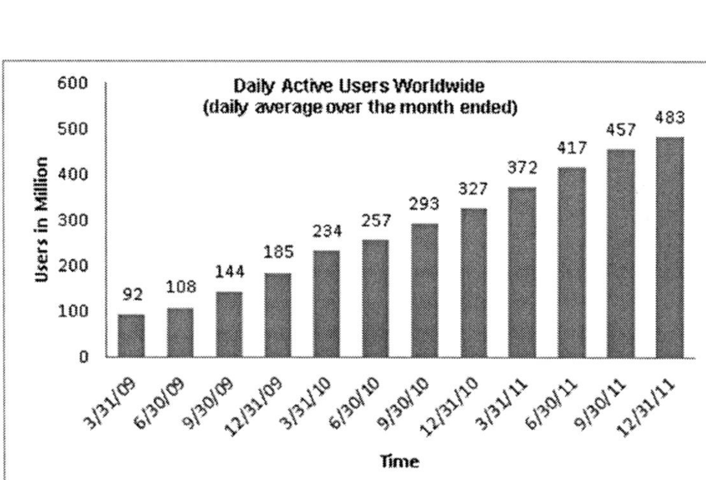

Figure 25: Facebook's Daily Active Users Worldwide
Source: Reproduction of United States Securities and Exchange Commission. (2011). Retrieved 09/04/2012, from http://sec.gov/Archives/edgar/data/1326801/000119312512034517/d287954ds1.htm.

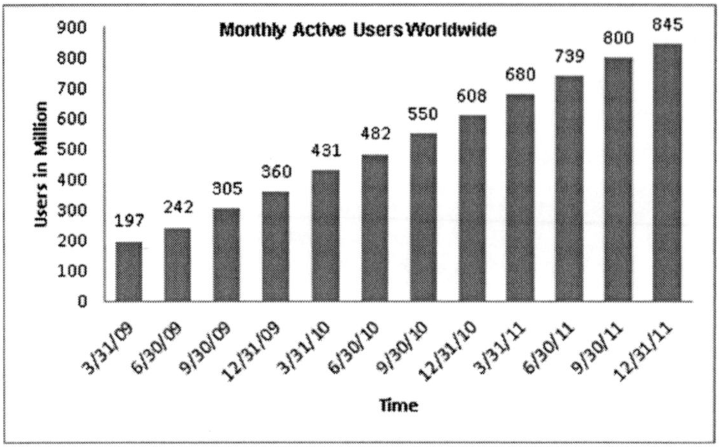

Figure 26: Facebook's Monthly Active Users Worldwide
Source: Reproduction of United States Securities and Exchange Commission. (2011). Retrieved 09/04/2012, from http://sec.gov/Archives/edgar/data/1326801/000119312512034517/d287954ds1.htm.

3.4.2 VKontakte

Вконтакте is the Russian spelling for VKontakte, which means "in connection" or "in contact". The mission of this social network, created in 2006 by Pavel Durov, is to help people to express their opinions and to find an audience. VKontakte is providing a communication platform to engage with a broad community of interesting people or keep in touch with friends and family. The aim is to remain the fastest, most modern and aesthetically pleasing means of communicating on the Internet. Since it represents striking similarities with Facebook, VKontakte is often seen as a so called "copycat" or even "Facebook clone". However, with more than 110 million registered users, VKontakte represents the most popular online social network in Russia, with over 70% of the registered users active in this country. This SNS is the most visited resource in the Russian Internet, enjoying growing popularity. Additional users mainly come from other CIS States (Commonwealth of Independent States). With an availability of 68 different languages, VKontakte aims to expand to other countries. Since it was launched, VKontakte benefitted from exponential growth. For instance in 2008, the number of users of this social network has risen from 3.5 million to nearly six million within five months (VKontakte 2012; Blog VK 2008).

3.4.3 Sina Weibo, Renren and Kaixin001

The development of the Chinese Internet industry over the past decade is impressive and the total number of users in this state is increasing at an enormous speed. By the beginning of 2012, the number of Internet users in China had reached more than 513 million, surpassing the U.S. as the world's largest Internet market. Along with the growth of the Internet in China and triggered

by the prohibition of a large number of Internet sites (Google, Facebook, Twitter, etc.), instant messaging tools as well as SNS arose. Considering the most popular SNS, Sina Weibo, Renren, and Kaixin001 encompass almost every aspect of Chinese social life (Yu, Asur & Huberman 2011: 2; State Council Information Office of the People's Republic of China 2010; Internet World Stats 2011; Fu and Wu 2011: 37; PSFK 2012; Endeshav 2004: 41).
The landscape of Chinese SNS is diverse and thriving. All providers are facing high competition in China and no single player is as dominant as Facebook in the U.S. Figure 27 outlines the long tail of networks for different users and different purposes for the top seven sites.

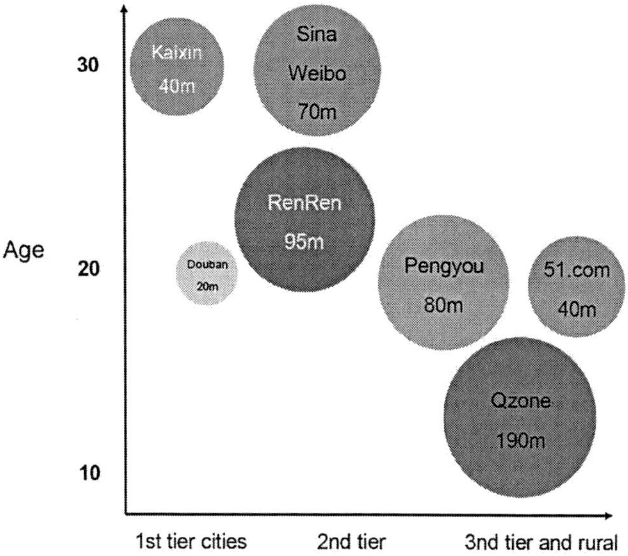

Figure 27: China's Social Network Universe
Source: Lukoff 2011b. Retrieved 10/04/2012, from
http://techrice.com/2011/03/08/chinas-top-15-social-networks.

In the following, Sina Weibo, Renren as well as Kaixin001 will be described. These social media sites are, due to their target group of mainly white collar workers, an attractive focus for globally operating companies (Offbeat China 2011; Lukoff 2011b).
In July 2009, the Sina Corporation launched China's biggest Web portal, the microblogging site Sina Weibo. With growing reputation, the Chinese microblogging clone of Twitter is increasing their user numbers, reaching over 300 million in the beginning of 2012. Therefore, Sina Weibo is becoming more and more interesting to investors and participants.
However, since the empirical case of this research is focusing on social networks with the aim of direct engagement, this SNS will not be applied in the example of BMW, adidas and NIVEA (chapter 5) (SinaWeibo 2011; Yu, Asur & Huberman 2011: 3-4; IT Times 2012: 1, Goldkorn 2011: 1).

Renren as well as Kaixin 001, two famous SNS in China, provide great convenience to communicate online. Renren (in Chinese: 人人, meaning "network for everybody") was founded in 2005 by Joseph Chen and signifies the earliest and leading real name SNS in China. Renren aims to optimise the social networking experience and to enable users to connect and communicate with others. Through features and services such as sharing information, generating content, playing online games, listening to music and shopping for deals, the way that Internet users connect should be revolutionised. Renren, often regarded as a clone of Facebook, is the most popular SNS among the Chinese youth. Anything Facebook releases is immediately copied by Renren: Connect, Like, Places, Groups, etc. (Renren 2012; Goldkorn 2011: 1; Lukoff 2011a, Offbeat China 2011).

Kaixin001 (in Chinese: ▪心网, meaning "Happy Net") was founded in 2008 and has about 100 million registered users. Kaixin001 mainly gained popularity amongst white collar workers via its social games and mail forwarding features. The site was the first one to copy and release the most successful Facebook applications Happy Farm and Friends for Sale. Kaixin001 is one of the biggest rivals of Renren in China. Even if its popularity is decreasing due to the rise of the microblogging platform Sina Weibo, it is still a crucial SNS mainly used in China's tier one cities, including the biggest metropolises like Shanghai and Beijing (Lukoff 2011b; Offbeat China 2011).

The Chinese social media space is diverse, thriving and in continuous movement. "Despite government regulations that make the Internet an "invisible birdcage", Chinese SNS have just enough space to fly" (Lukoff 2011a: 2). Diverse applications and services on the Internet have provided a broader scope for people to represent their interests and express their opinions. The challenge to participate in the virtual world of the BRIC countries has encouraged many globally operating companies to increase their digital activities (Huberman 2011: 3). The following chapter introduces the empirical investigation of the case studies of BMW, adidas and NIVEA, which are active in the SNS of BRIC.

4 Empirical Investigation

The increased complexity of the business environment today leads to a higher relevance of market research. In general, market research consists of the systematic and objective gathering and processing of information about markets and customers. Whenever markets are about to change, situations are fluctuating or competition intensifies, effective market research often is of substantial importance (McQuarrie 2006: ix; Malhotra 2007: 7). Within this study about social media marketing in BRIC countries, BMW, adidas and NIVEA will be focused on and analysed as an example for globally operating German companies in the following SNS: Facebook in Brazil and India, VKontakte in Russia and Renren and Kaixin001 in China. This chapter outlines the empirical investigation of this study and starts with a description of the three investigated companies BMW, adidas and NIVEA and why they have been selected. Afterwards, the chosen methodological approach combining quantitative and qualitative methods is introduced. The methods applied in the research of this study, namely expert interviews, quantitative analyses of companies as well as a user survey, will be outlined and explained in the subsequent chapters.

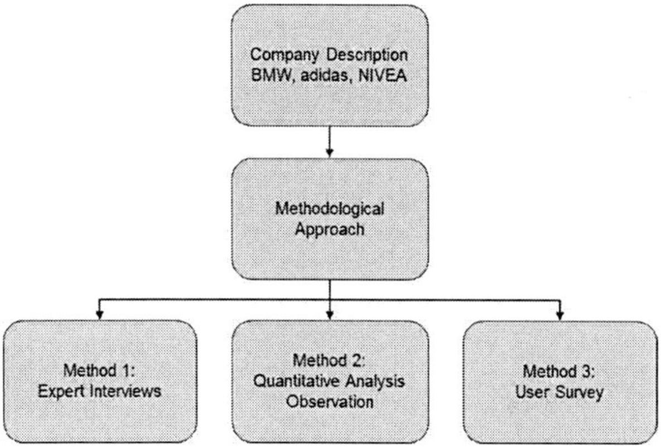

Figure 28: Structure of Chapter 4
Source: Own Illustration.

4.1 BMW, adidas and NIVEA

The activity of companies in SNS of the BRIC countries was examined for the globally operating German enterprises BMW, adidas and NIVEA.

BMW together with MINI, and Rolls-Royce Motor Cars belongs to the BMW Group, which focuses on the premium segment of the international automobile industry. With these three, belonging to the strongest premium brands in the automobile branch, the BMW Group is one of Germany's largest industrial companies. BMW, "Bayrische Motoren Werke" GmbH, was

founded in 1916 and became BMW AG in 1918. BMW AG, the main brand of the BMW Group, is responsible for 84% of all sales (BMW Group 2010; BMW Group 2012).
The adidas AG was founded in 1949. The adidas Group is made up of the brands adidas itself, Reebok and TayloreMade. This German company is leader in the sporting goods industry and offers a broad portfolio of products. In virtually every country of the world, products from the adidas Group are available. Adidas AG as a parent company of adidas Group is stated to be the second largest sporting goods manufacturer of the world (adidas Group 2011; adidas 2012).
NIVEA, a globally operating German brand, founded in 1911, is the most known and an important brand of the Beiersdorf AG. The brand NIVEA includes diverse products concerning body care such as lotions or cremes. In view of their revenue, NIVEA is seen as the world biggest brand regarding skin care (NIVEA 2012; NIVEA 2010).
BMW, adidas and NIVEA were chosen for several reasons. All brands are somehow present in the SNS of the BRIC countries. All three German brands have a long tradition and are globally established. Moreover, according to globeone (2011: 324), they belong to the spontaneously remembered German brands in the BRIC population. Within the automotive sector, one of Germany's most traditional and famous industries, BMW is stated as the best known German brand with 89 % awareness in BRIC countries. Adidas is following with 85% awareness in BRIC and NIVEA with 74%. Moreover, considering the best-liked German brands, BMW is leading again with 84%. With regard to the most frequently purchased and used German brands, adidas (60%), followed by NIVEA (51%), hold the first two places. Additionally, the investigated brands were chosen, since "the vast majority of urban BRIC population has a positive attitude towards German brands" (globeone 2011: 3). Furthermore, German brands in general are favored over for example Japanese, US American, French or Chinese ones. "This perception is especially distinctive for traditional values like reliability, quality and trustworthiness" (globeone 2011: 3). Another advantage of this sample is the diversity of the represented goods: automotive, skin care and sport products. The aspect that B2C companies are rather active in SNS than B2B ones (Stelzner 2010: 22) was confirmed by several social media experts. For consumer goods, meaning B2C, there is no other way than being active in SNS (Interview V 2012: 8; Interview IV 2012: 6-9).
Before discussing the results of the empirical investigation in chapter 5, the chosen methods concerning the data collection and analysis will be presented in the course of this chapter.

4.2 Methodological Approach

In order to find out about the activity and presence of the companies BMW, adidas and NIVEA in the SNS of the BRIC countries, primary as well as secondary research has been conducted during the first quarter of 2012. Concerning the latter, data and research findings discussed in books, scientific journals, magazines, databases, etc. were studied. Additionally, websites and blogs provided further insights about social media.
With regard to the primary research, the current study is based on different empirical investigation methods, exploratory/ qualitative as well as quantitative research. "Microsoft Excel" was used to evaluate the quantitative results. In the following, an overview of the chosen approach is shown.

Approaches	Methods
Exploratory/ Qualitative	Expert interviews
Quantitative	User survey
	Quantitative analysis of companies' engagement in social networks

Table 4: Approaches and Methods of the Empirical Investigation
Source: Own Illustration.

Qualitative research explores a situation to provide insights about a studied context. An important characteristic is its flexibility. Qualitative methods include interviews, participant observation, and group discussions. Small samples provide insights and a deeper understanding of the studied context, including for example general thoughts, feelings or usage patterns.
In quantitative research, numeric data are gathered, in order analyse the data statistically. Techniques which can be used in quantitative research, include Internet surveys, mail surveys or the specific count of data (Malhotra 2007: 80-82, 143; Malhotra and Birks 2006: 132-133).
In the following chapters, the respective methods and their application in the context of this research will be outlined.

4.2.1 Expert Interviews

The method of a personal interview belongs to the exploratory qualitative research procedures. Compared to other forms of interviews, expert interviews directly focus on the knowledge of the person. An expert is a person representative of an organisation or institution who has privileged access to information and special knowledge (Malhotra 2007: 186; Bogner, Littig and Menz 2005:39-42). The objective of the researcher is to reconstruct this knowledge during an interview. In the following empirical investigation, six social media and marketing experts were interviewed by telephone. One of the major advantages was that sensitive information could be accessed directly. The interviews took place during a time span of about two weeks (12 March 2012 – 30 March 2012) and had an average length of about 45 minutes. The interviews were transcribed and sent back to the experts for approval, who all agreed to be cited in the context of this study (Bogner, Littig & Menz 2005: 39, 113-114).
Although all experts received an interview guideline in order to be familiar with the questions and the direction of the interview beforehand, the interview questions varied, if new aspects were brought up as a new issue. Concerning the structure of the guideline (appendix b), the interview was divided into four parts. First of all, basic information about the expert was asked for. In the following section, basic knowledge about social media was inquired, whereas the third part focused on social media marketing in more detail. The last part emphasised social media marketing in BRIC countries. The motivated experts contributed valuable insights regarding the research topic. In order to be able to compare the interviews, the guidelines followed the same order. The findings from the expert interviews were directly included in the overall discussion of findings (chapter 5).

4.2.2 Quantitative Analysis of Companies' Engagement in Social Networks

Through the method of participant observation, the researcher is observing a context, in order to collect information. In this case, the analysis took place in a descriptive and quantitative manner, since numerical information was obtained. The method of undisguised observation was executed, which means that the respondents were aware that they were being observed (Malhotra 2007: 202). In social networks, members are responsible for their private settings and can determine how much information is shared with the public.

Within this research, the author examined the presence of these public groups and pages in the SNS of the BRIC countries. The objective was to collect the number of sites from BMW, adidas and NIVEA in SNS of BRIC. The numerical data were counted on the 8th of March 2012. In all observed BRIC SNS, pages and groups were counted and ordered according to participant numbers (appendices i, j, k). Additionally, statements about BMW, adidas and NIVEA in BRIC SNS were collected.

4.2.3 User Survey

The objective of a survey is to inquire information through a set of questions which are specific and standardised (Malhotra 2007: 184-186, 299-301). Therefore, users of the SNS of the BRIC countries were asked to analyse the activity of BMW, adidas and NIVEA on the company's official SNS. Through quota sampling, people were selected based on different factors, ensuring that participants were registered within the examined networks. Since the focus was put on the overall and general opinion of people within these SNS, sex and age were of no relevance.

The survey was divided in three interdependent parts including ten questions in total. At first, basic information about respondents was inquired, followed in the second part by questions about the approaches, appearance, and the activity of the respective brand in the BRIC SNS. A potential cultural adaption on the company SNS and suggestions for improvement were evaluated in the third section.

The fact that the users were informed by looking at the concerning pages before answering reduced the inability and unwillingness to answer. With the help of the Web survey tool "SurveyMonkey", the online questionnaire could be accessed by respondents in between 1 March and 13 April 2012. The following table gives an overview of the represented brands in BRIC SNS and their respective official country sites. SNS users were asked to look at these country-specific brand sites of the SNS they were using before filling in the questionnaire.

Considering the collection process, every third person found in the examined SNS was selected. This ensured the same chance for members to be selected eliminating researchers' bias.

The surveys were sent out to 120 people, registered in the respective network, meaning 30 surveys per country. All participants were given the same message and explanation, in order to fill in the survey. The results were evaluated in the end and can be found in appendix m. The main results are discussed in chapter 5.

Country	Network	Brand	Page
Brazil	Facebook	BMW	http://www.facebook.com/BMWBrasil?ref=ts
		adidas	http://www.facebook.com/BMWBrasil?ref=ts#!/pages/ADIDAS-BRASIL/127659200670383
		NIVEA	http://www.facebook.com/BMWBrasil?ref=ts#!/niveabrasil
Russia	VKontakte	BMW	http://vk.com/bmw_drive
		adidas	http://vk.com/id165953519#/Adidas_515
		NIVEA	http://vk.com/id165953519#/nivea
India	Facebook	BMW	http://www.facebook.com/pages/Adidas-India/309602937582#!/bmwindia
		adidas	http://www.facebook.com/pages/Adidas-India/121631571274446
		NIVEA	http://www.facebook.com/pages/Adidas-India/309602937582#!/NIVEA.in
China	Renren/ Kaixin001	BMW	http://www.kaixin001.com/home/?uid=58797480
		adidas	http://page.renren.com/Adidasoriginals
		NIVEA	http://www.kaixin001.com/home/?uid=83741102

Table 5: Examined SNS in BRIC Countries
Source: Own Illustration.

5 The Cases of BMW, adidas and NIVEA in SNS of the BRIC Countries

In this chapter, the results of quantitative and qualitative research of this study will be presented and discussed. Initially, the focus lies on analysing the conducted survey, referring to the before mentioned theories in chapter 2. The general activity of BMW, adidas and NIVEA regarding marketing via SNS will be outlined and finally, best practice suggestions will be presented. All analyses are combined with statements of the interviewed experts and the social media theories.

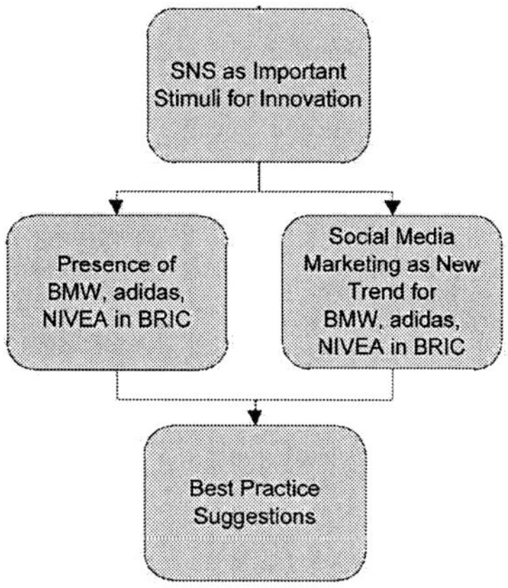

Figure 29: Structure of Chapter 5
Source: Own Illustration.

5.1 Digital Social Networks as Important Stimuli for Information

Networks in general are offering the opportunity to get and stay in touch with friends, family or others via the creation of a personal profile. The reason why people are participating in SNS seems clear to social media expert Schöllhammer (Interview I 2012: 2):

> Why are people talking? Social media is mainly about generating content. And the main aspect of social media is to have conversations and the dialogue between people. So, the question is why people are talking?

This point has also been emphasised by other social media experts, outlining the desire of SNS users to communicate, socialise, talk and to stay in contact with others (Interview II 2012: 2; Interview V 2012: 2). Kopka (Interview IV 2012: 2), Vice President of the social network XING, is even linking the aspect of people using SNS with Aristoteles, stating that the human is a social being: "Nach Aristoteles ist der Mensch ein soziales Wesen". Kopka describes social media as a tool which is satisfying the human basic need of communication. According to Buchanan (Interview III 2012: 2), people are using social media in order to position themselves. Social media would diplay a virtual picture of daily life, "das virtuelle Abbild des ganz normalen Lebens" (Interview III 2012: 2). Due to this basic need of communication, the exchange of information between people is taking place. Within the SNS, this exchange is realized via the tools provided by the different sites. Since social networks are simple tools for staying in touch with work contacts, friends, and extended family, most SNS users operate with larger social networks, i.e. are connected to a lot of people, not only closest contacts. This aspect was discussed by all interviewed social media experts, stating for example that in social networks a lot of people are called friends, although the relationship intensity is frequently low (Interview III 2012: 3). Nevertheless, it is mainly assumed that the networks consist of rather homogenous groups of people. "Die Information, die Ihr enges Netzwerk hat, ist wahrscheinlich relativ identisch. [...] Da hat wahrscheinlich keiner eine Königsinformation" (Interview IV 2012: 5; Burt 2004: 349-352).

In the context of this study, the author operates from the premise that SNS mainly consist of weak ties, since the majority of people are connected to an extended circle of friends. Granovetter outlines that through rather weak connections between people, the flow of information is increased (Granovetter 1973). These weak ties can connect different groups and therefore overcome structural holes. According to Burt, this leads to the creation of new knowledge since non-redundant contacts are exchanging information between rather homogenous groups (Burt 2004: 350). Therefore, it can be concluded that the speed of information as well as the creation of new knowledge is enormous within these SNS and increasing further with its enlargement.

> [W]hatever is to be diffused can reach a larger number of people, and traverse greater social distance (i.e., path length), when passed through weak ties rather than strong (Granovetter 1973: 1366).

These aspects are taken by Grabher and Maintz (2007: 190), also seeing the potential of the weak SNS ties as "important stimuli for innovation". Other advantages to companies when operating in social media were examined by a survey of Stelzner (2010: 15): He found that "[...] 85% of all marketers indicated that their social media efforts have generated exposure for their businesses". Improving traffic was the second major benefit he identified, followed by building new partnerships. Additionally, more than 50% of marketers outlined the benefits of social media marketing in the generation of qualified leads.

It will be examined and discussed in the following chapters of this study, if BMW, adidas and NIVEA are also taking advantage of these benefits. First, their SNS approaches will be outlined.

5.2 The Presence of BMW, adidas and NIVEA in SNS of the BRIC Countries

In order to demonstrate how social media marketing is conducted by companies, BMW, adidas and NIVEA were chosen as case studies. The following paragraphs show general results of the evaluation. They serve as a basis for the ongoing discussion.

In total, 105 people from BRIC answered the user survey "Social media marketing in BRIC countries" (appendix l, m). They provided general insights and personal opinions about various aspects of the social media appearance of the three chosen companies. The division of survey participants by country is shown in figure 30.

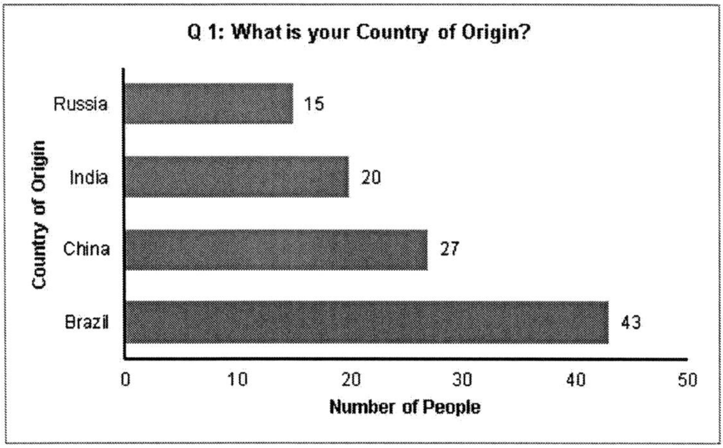

Figure 30: Division of Participants by Country
Source: Own Illustration.

The majority of people with about 40% of survey respondents came from Brazil, followed by China with 25%, India with 20% and Russia with 15%. In terms of evaluated brands active in SNS, the majority of respondents focused on adidas with about 40%, followed by NIVEA with 35% and BMW with 25%. The division can be seen in the following chart, figure 31.

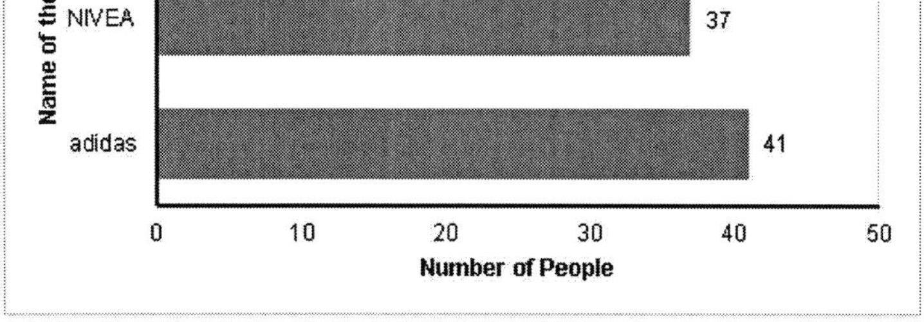

Figure 31: Divisions of Brands
Source: Own Illustration.

Using a Pivot table, the countries and brands were set in relation to each other and the following results were obtained (figure 32).

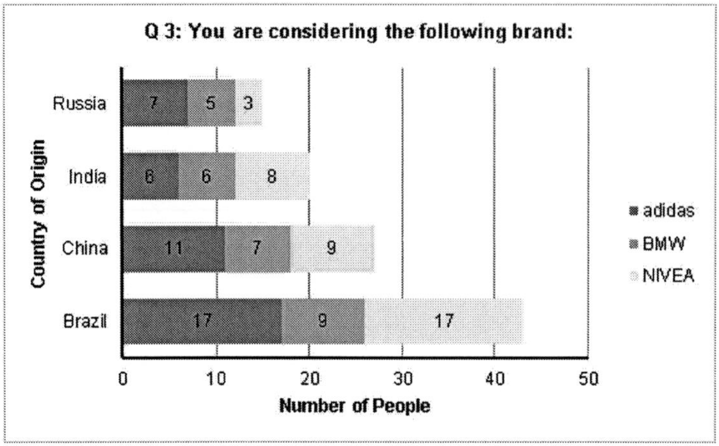

Figure 32: Combination of Countries and Brands
Source: Own Illustration.

Social networks allow its members to create their personalised page, for example by posting specific pictures, sharing certain content or updating their recent locations. Within SNS it is also possible for members to become fan of a brand, receive news as well as to interact on the respective page, e.g. by way of commenting.

A lot of people are not only becoming a fan of company pages, but even create own pages or groups, in order to express thoughts about chosen subjects. On these pages, other people are able to interact and share their opinions.

The quantitative analysis of BMW, adidas and NIVEA examined the following aspects:

1. The numbers of groups and pages of the studied brands in each BRIC country.
2. The number of liked pages and group members of the studied brands in each BRIC country.
3. The largest page of each brand in the respective SNS.

Within SNS, groups consist of members, whereas the participation on a page is indicated by liking the page. In the context of this study, 'Sites' and 'Participants' will be used to combine the following meanings:

- Groups + Pages → Sites
- Members + Likes → Participants

All examinations in the form of tables can be found in the appendix. The most important findings will be outlined and discussed in the course of the subsequent chapters.

Figure 33 shows the aggregate numbers of sites within the most relevant SNS of each BRIC country for BMW:

- Facebook for Brazil and India,
- VKontakte for Russia,
- Kaixin001 and Renren for China.

Since BMW, adidas and NIVEA all showed a similar distribution pattern in terms their numbers of pages in SNS of BRIC, BMW was chosen as the prime example to outline the common trend.

The dominance of the numbers of SNS in Russia, nearly accounts for 100% of the total number of all the sites in BRIC combined (figure 33).

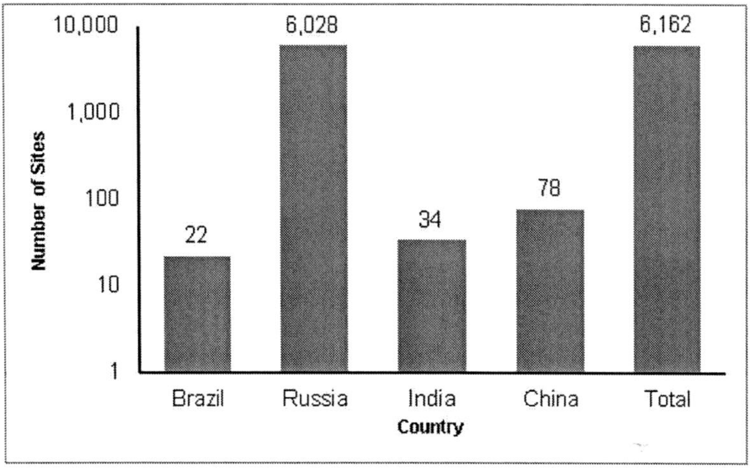

Figure 33: Numbers of Sites in the SNS of BRIC – BMW
Source: Own Illustration.

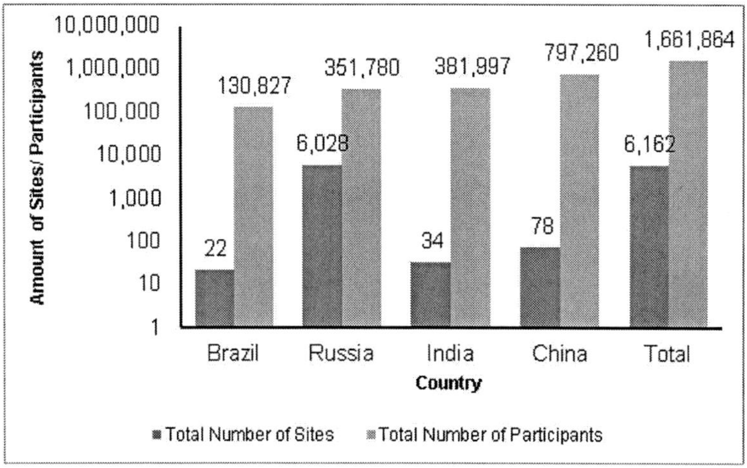

Figure 34: Comparison of Sites and Participants – BMW
Source: Own Illustration.

In comparison to this, Brazil, India and China are lacking behind and create the impression to hardly have any presence in the examined SNS market. However, when analysing the number of participants and setting it in relation to the total number of sites (figure 34), another meaning will be derived from the data.

Through this comparison, it becomes obvious that even a small number of sites within a SNS does not indicate a lot about its participants.

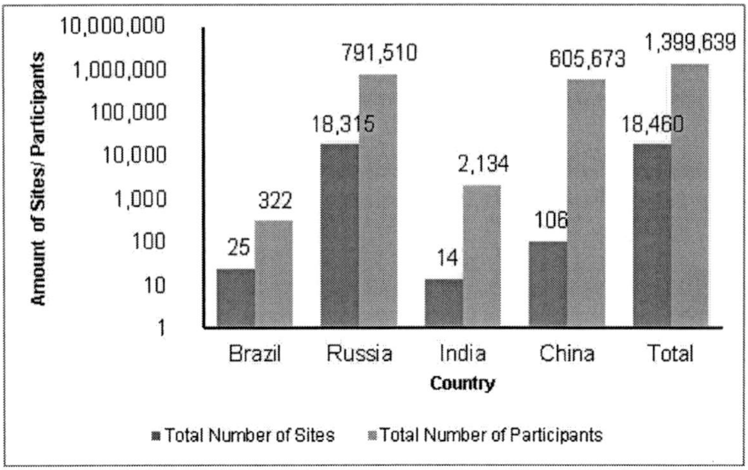

Figure 35: Comparison of Sites and Participants – adidas
Source: Own Illustration.

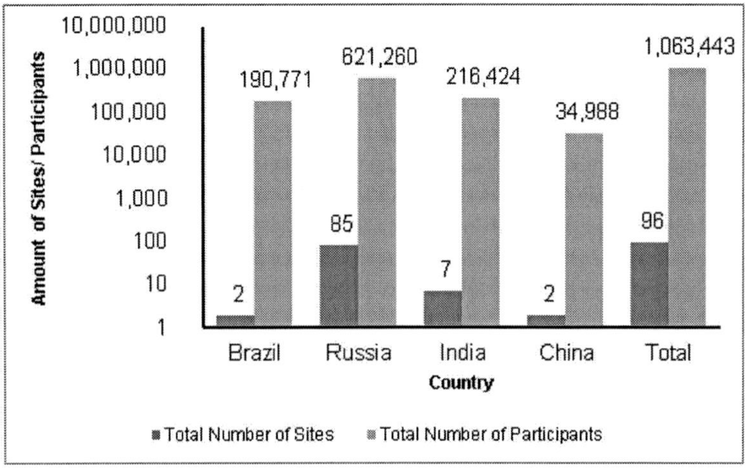

Figure 36: Comparison of Sites and Participants – NIVEA
Source: Own Illustration.

To illustrate this with an example, China's number of sites only accounts for around 1% of the total number of sites. However, within this 1% of sites, the number of participants is really high

and represents 50% of total participants. Compared to Russia, which is almost entirely responsible for the total number of sites as discussed before (figure 33), they just represent around 20% of participants.
Comparing the numbers of sites and participants, similar distribution patterns for the three brands BMW, NIVEA and adidas are visible. The following graphs (figure 35 and 36) outline the results for NIVEA and adidas.
Setting the number of sites and number of participants for BMW, adidas and NIVEA in comparison to each other, the combined table can be derived:

Brand	Total Numbers of Sites in BRIC	Total Numbers of Participants in BRIC
BMW	6,162	1,661,864
adidas	18,460	1,399,639
NIVEA	96	1,063,443

Table 6: Total Numbers of Sites and Participants in BRIC
Source: Own Illustration.

With regards to the total numbers of sites in BRIC, adidas is the leader with over 18,000 sites followed by BMW with more than 6,000 and NIVEA with less than 100 sites. It could be argued that adidas' strategy to attract the attention of the audience in SNS is working pretty well, since people are creating own sites directly related to adidas. This leads to the assumption that adidas as a brand is already well established in Brazil, Russia, India and China and social network members are actively creating sites for this brand.
Concerning BMW, which is representing a premium brand, the reason for a lower creation of separate sites could be explained by the economic situation of the SNS users in BRIC. It is possible that only a small percentage of users are able to afford buying a premium car and are therefore not interested in creating sites for this product.
With regards to NIVEA, the results with less than 100 total created sites in BRIC compared to the other two brands were poor. From this observation, it can be assumed that NIVEA is not yet established in the BRIC countries, possibly due to lacking appropriate strategy. People are not awar of the brand and therefore not interested in creating related sites within social networks.
However, concerning the participants within SNS, more than one million were counted for each brand (table 6). BMW with more than 1.5 million participants within their SNS sites is leading the group of the examined brands. With around 1.4 and 1.1 million participants, adidas and NIVEA are following.
Therefore, it can be concluded that even with a small number of sites, the number of participants can be relatively high (comp. adidas, table 6, figure 35).
Here, the question arises, if it is more beneficial to a company to be represented by

a. a large number of sites relating to the company but each with a smaller number of participants or by
b. a rather small number of sites, but with a high number of participants.

Due to the desire of people to communicate, to engage in dialogue and to share content (Interviews 1-6), the latter variant seems to be more valuable due to a higher number of participants

in the same place. Even in a small number of network sites, where a lot of people are participating, more content is being shared and more people are able to interact and form part of an ongoing discussion.
In order to find out more details regarding this assumption, the author further refined and evaluated the data. Hence, the number of participants of the largest site of each brand were identified and set in relation to the whole number of participants within its SNS. The objective here was to identify how many of the total participants belong to the largest site.
The following three graphs directly compare the numbers of total participants and can be relatively compared to the number of participants of the largest site. This is indicated by a proportion in percentage. As outlined in the figures 37 and 38, BMW and NIVEA show a similar distribution pattern, whereby in all BRIC countries, except Russia- BMW, nearly all participants belong to the largest site. This indicates that in the SNS of BRIC, mainly one group is dominant, where the vast majority of people is participating.
Russia, as outlined before (table 6), is by far the leader concerning the number of sites. Since every site here only consists of a few members, no main pages can be found for Russia BMW.
When referring to adidas, the situation presents a slightly different picture. On average, less than 50% of the total number of participants in BRIC belong to the largest site (figure 39). This means that main conversations around adidas are not focused on one page but rather distributed among different ones. As a result, lower engagement and lower awareness can be expected.

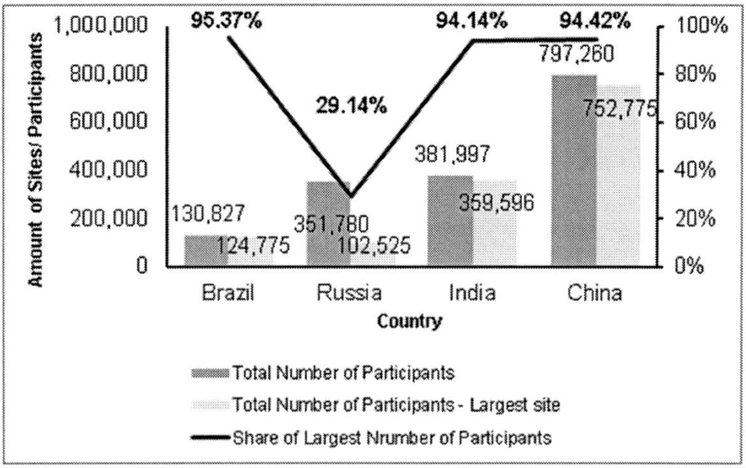

Figure 37: Comparison of Participants at All Sites/ the Largest Site – BMW
Source: Own Illustration.

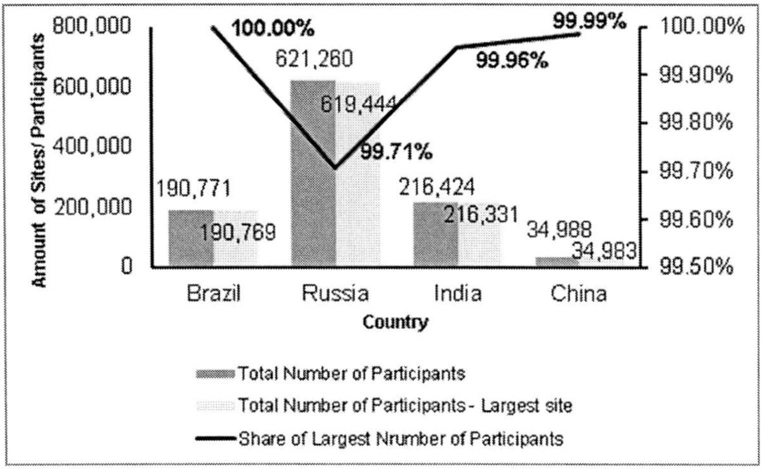

Figure 38: Comparison of Participants at All Sites/ the Largest Site – NIVEA
Source: Own Illustration.

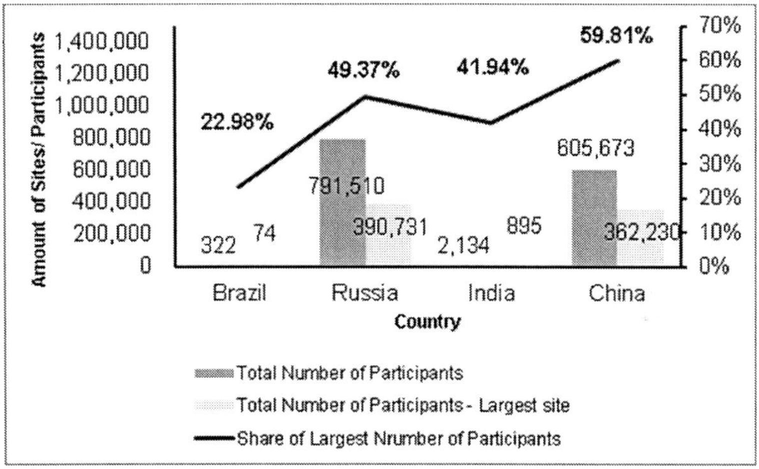

Figure 39: Comparison of Participants at All Sites/ the Largest Site – adidas
Source: Own Illustration.

This could imply that even if adidas has a lot of people creating pages within the SNS of the BRIC countries (figure 35), the company itself has not yet been successful to attract the attention of the majority of their customers to their largest site.

Nevertheless, companies are more and more interested in using SNS for marketing purposes. This aspect will be outlined and analysed in the following chapter.

5.3 Social Media Marketing as a New Focus for BMW, adidas and NIVEA

The increasing use of social media around the world is recognised by companies, willing to expand their marketing strategies to include social media marketing and starting to establish presences within SNS. The majority of marketers have just started to use social media as a marketing instrument (Stelzner 2010: 11-23; Interview V 2012: 5-6).

If we consider the results presented in the last chapters, personal commitment leads people to take the initiative, create SNS pages and start discussions about specific topics such as BMW, adidas and NIVEA (chapter 5.2). This often happens before the companies themselves established a presence. Therefore, one should ask the question, if the companies have not already missed the opportunity to become a part of this "revolution".

> Viele Firmen haben diesen Punkt einfach schon verpennt und heute bezahlen sie dann viel Geld, um sich Rat zu holen, wie die ihre Firma einfach ein bisschen präsenter in den sozialen Netzwerken machen können (Interview III 2012: 6).

Often people who created such a SNS page don't receive the appropriate and necessary recognition by companies. Most companies don't even realize their presence in the virtual world. The only thing which is clear is that companies nowadays should be present within the market of the future: social media (Interview II 2012: 2).

> In previous times, you had to be on the "Yellow Pages" to be found, then on Google and now the presence in social networks like Facebook is required to be found. So, without any question, you have to be present nowadays in social media and active in social networks. The only question is: How do I present myself? (Interview I 2012: 3).

How BMW, adidas and NIVEA represent themselves in the SNS of the BRIC countries can be seen in the following graph, figure 40. The participants of the survey stated their opinions about the social media appearances of the examined brands.

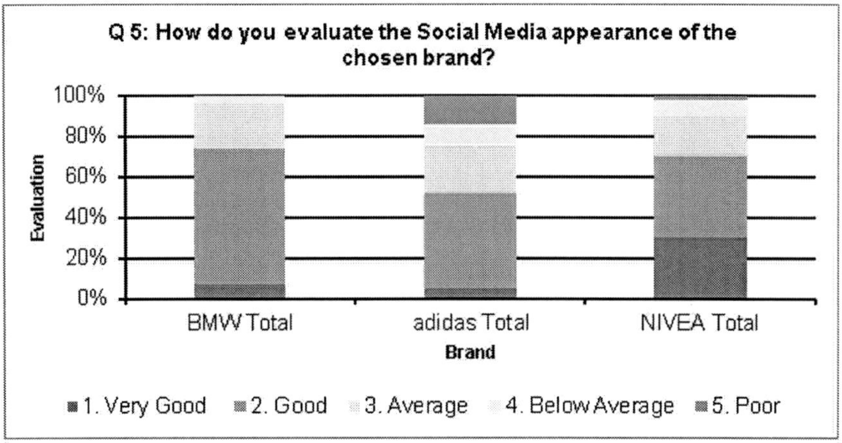

Figure 40: Social Media Appearances in BRIC – BMW, adidas and NIVEA
Source: Own Illustration.

BMW was awarded with almost 80% reviews and NIVEA with around 60% of reviews that were at least good. However, this case is not applicable for adidas, where the social media appearance was considered between average to poor by half of the participants.
The social media appearance of BMW in Brazil (figure 42) will be more closely analysed at the end of this chapter, also including statements of its social media analyst, Jorge Junior (Interview VI appendix h). In order to examine differences between the SNS in each BRIC country, the analysis was broken down in more detail and the results analysed further.

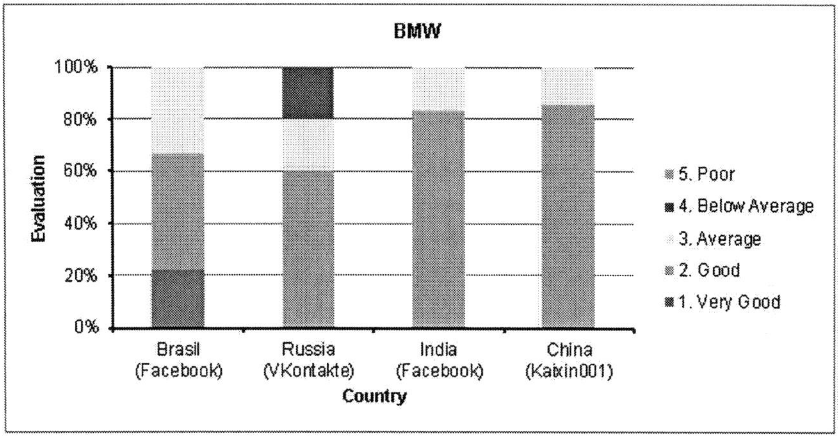

Figure 41: Social Media Appearance in BRIC – BMW
Source: Own Illustration.

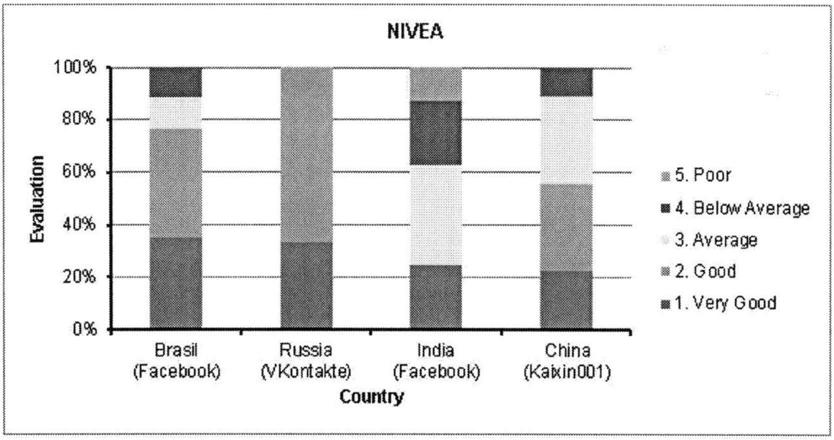

Figure 42: Social Media Appearance in BRIC – NIVEA
Source: Own Illustration.

In nearly all SNS, NIVEA was graded 3 and 4, representing average and below average performance (figure 42). In India, more than 70% of participants evaluated NIVEA on Facebook as being a low performer, between average and poor. Although there exists a page created by NIVEA India Facebook, there is no live activity to create engagement.

This missing activity can also be recognised in the case of adidas (figure 43). An official active presence in Brazil and India is missing, indicating low engagement levels.

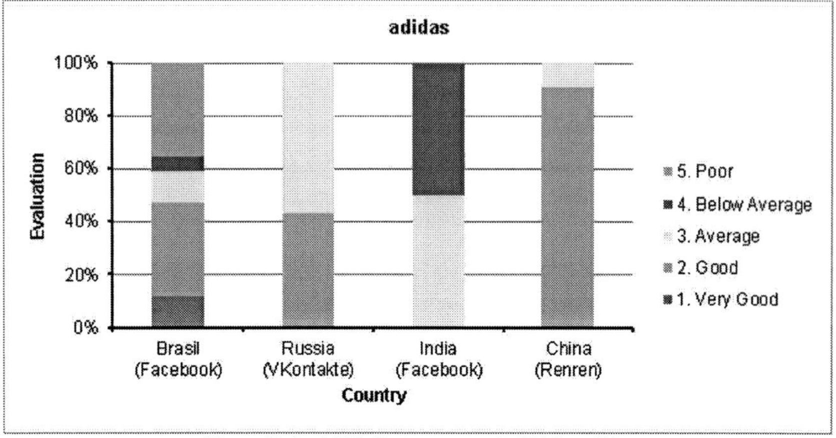

Figure 43: Social Media Appearance in BRIC – adidas
Source: Own Illustration.

Even if adidas represents the highest number of created sites within the BRIC Countries (table 6), it lacks active participation in growing the brand. This means that adidas is likely to face challenges and risks in order to adapt to their customer base, especially in Brazil and India.

Since companies have to be where their customers are (according to Kopka, Interview IV 2012: 3), they have to be active in social media. In accordance with Wöllenstein (Interview V 2012: 3), social media is the buzzword of our time. Nevertheless, Wöllenstein is approaching this topic with scepticism, stating that a lot of companies are just participating in social media, because they think that they have to follow this trend. Therefore, they are overlooking their actual objective to focus on their target group. It is necessary for companies to be active in social media, but with the right strategy. Pages with no activity even lead to a worse outcome than no presence at all.

> Also Social Media hört man ja überall. Das ist das Schlagwort. Ich bin in der Hinsicht ein wenig skeptisch, weil ich denke, dass es ganz toll, ganz modern ist und ganz viele Unternehmen einfach darauf anspringen, weil es einfach schick ist. Und für heute gesprochen glaube ich, dass viele Unternehmen irgendwas machen, weil sie glauben es machen zu müssen, unabhängig davon, ob die Zielgruppe, die sie eigentlich ansprechen, dafür geeignet ist (Interview V 2012: 3).

The SNS activity of BMW, adidas and NIVEA varies across the examined SNS in the BRIC countries (figure 44).

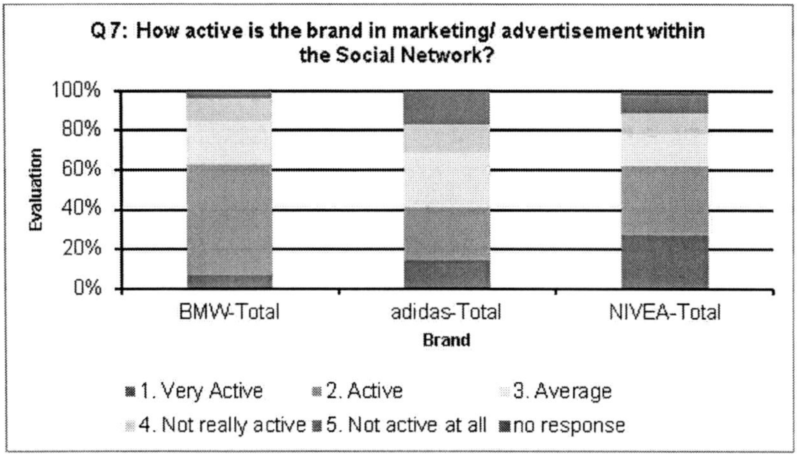

Figure 44: Social Media Activity in BRIC – BMW, adidas and NIVEA
Source: Own Illustration.

With regard to their activity within the examined SNS, BMW and NIVEA performed best. Keeping in mind that adidas India, adidas Brazil and NIVEA India are not really present in these SNS (see figures 42 and 44), negative user evaluations in these cases are not surprising. About 60% of the participants just evaluated the activity of adidas as average or worse.

Concerning the appearance of social media in general, and in particular social networks, BMW constitutes an exemplary case (figure 40 and 41). Regarding BMW's social media strategy in Brazil, Jorge Junior, marketing analyst and responsible for the social media presence of BMW Brazil, provided some insights (Interview VI 2012: 2-4). According to Junior, social media is the future. The biggest chance for BMW Brazil is monitoring.

> [H]ere we can directly learn from the people and our customers. We are really active. We can stay directly engaged with our customers, because they are telling us, if they are happy or not (Interview VI 2012: 2).

Through their SNS presence and activity, BMW Brazil wants to inform people about their premium products. Hereby, also the interaction between the different departments plays an important role.

> So if we talk about some technical information, we also speak before with the engineers. And if someone has questions about jobs, they will communicate via social media to the human resources. So through our page you stay in contact with the other departments (Interview VI 2012: 3).

BMW Brazil tries its best to adapt to the Brazilian cultural context, for example by targeting people in Brazil's main language Portuguese. This is done in order to reach the vast majority of their target group and not to cause any avoidable misunderstandings. Junior states that "we have global content when telling people all about the brand, but it's always locally adapted" (Interview VI 2012: 4).

As it will be outlined later in this chapter, the local adaption is also desired by the majority of participants. Junior also mentioned that this engagement with customers would be very valuable for the company.
However, more than 80% of the participants of the survey are expecting a greater commitment in terms of engagement from the three brands BMW, adidas and NIVEA in their SNS of the BRIC countries. This can be seen in figure 45.

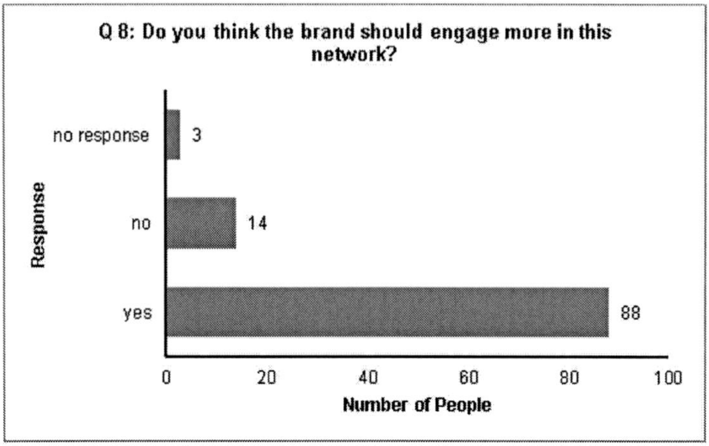

Figure 45: Engagement in SNS of BRIC – BMW, adidas and NIVEA
Source: Own Illustration.

Company engagement seems to be one of the most important aspects for participants. The fact to directly receive feedback constitutes a unique selling point of social networks. More suggestions for improvement were made by the survey participants and will be explained in the context of the following chapter.

5.4 Best Practice Suggestions for BMW, adidas and NIVEA

As soon as companies decide to participate in social networks and want to become active with their own company site, the right strategy seems indispensable. In accordance with Wöllenstein (Interview V 2012: 8), in the near future all companies will have to think about how to deal with the topic of social media. Companies have to adapt their social media strategy to their target group. The "traditional values" of having an objective, examining the actual situation and then creating a strategy always have to be kept in mind (Interview IV 2012: 7-8). A "customised strategy" (Interview II 2012: 3) is necessary.
Within their strategy, companies should think about the approaches to attract a large number of customers. Considering BMW, adidas and NIVEA, the following graph shows an overall picture of their tactics within their SNS.
All companies made use of the local languages and national figures and celebrities in advertisements. The integration of local traditions and famous national sights of the BRIC countries

were the next popular marketing approaches (see figure 46 above). The importance of adapting online marketing strategies to the local context is also supported by Interviewee VI.

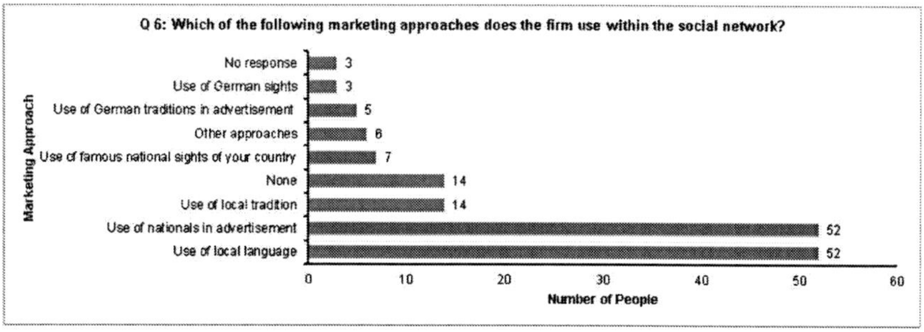

Figure 46: Marketing Approaches in SNS of BRIC – BMW, adidas and NIVEA
Source: Own Illustration.

Local elements of the country-of-origin of the firms BMW, adidas and NIVEA, i.e. German sights or German traditions were not utilised in the online presences. Although globeone (2011: 3-24) found out in their "BRIC Branding Survey" that in general German brands are favoured over brands from for example France or the U.S., BMW, adidas and NIVEA did not focus on the representation of a German image.

Here the question arises, if German companies, active in BRIC, could increase their marketing effect by way of paying more attention to their origin. Traditional German values such as reliability, quality and trustworthiness (globeone 2011: 3) could be presented within the SNS of the three brands.

Nevertheless, the vast majority of the interviewed BRIC population is already aware of multiple German brands, whereby BMW is taking the pole position with 89% of awareness and adidas with 85%. Moreover, adidas and NIVEA represent the most frequently purchased German brands within the BRIC countries (globeone 2011: 4-24).

Concerning the aspect that people already know the country of origin of BMW, adidas and NIVEA, it would therefore be better to focus more on other approaches. This point is also confirmed by Junior, stating that

> everybody knows that it's a German brand, so here we are more adapting to the culture as in terms of language. We don't push that BMW is German. I would say that we have much more than just being German (Interview VI 2012: 4).

The majority of survey participants also expressed that companies should adapt their advertisement more to the country they are operating in (figure 47).

The necessity to adapt to the respective culture also seems clear to social media experts as locality would play an increasing role (Interview IV 2012: 3). Since social media is just a picture of reality, companies have to adapt to the cultures where they are operating in and find out how people are living. "[W]ie man im realen Leben handelt, so sollte man natürlich dann auch im sozialen Netzwerk handeln" (Interview III 2012: 6). Within SNS, this adaption could take place by creating several pages for each country with a deeper focus on the cultural background (Interview V 2012: 6-8; Interview II 2012: 5). Through local pages, cultural misunderstandings could be avoided. In addition to the local presences, companies should also have a global, superior existence in the SNS (Interview IV 2012: 8; Interview I 2012: 7).

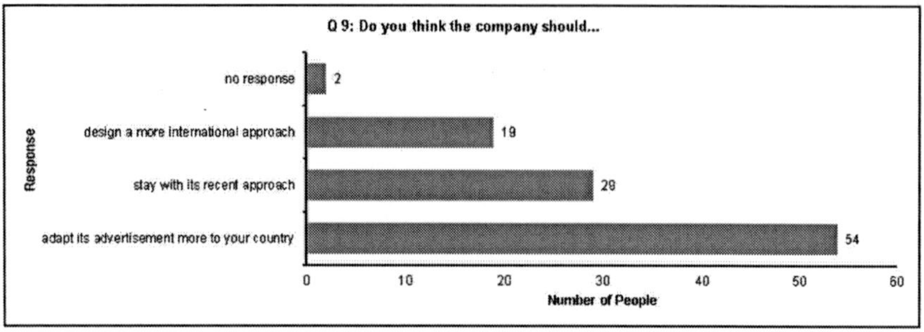

Figure 47: Potential Approach – BMW, adidas and NIVEA
Source: Own Illustration.

BMW, adidas and NIVEA all have an official company page in the SNS of the BRIC countries. However, considering the overall performance of the three brands, BMW and NIVEA are outperforming adidas in terms of higher activity levels within their SNS (figures 40 and 45).
Even if this adaption process towards localisation is one of the major challenges, it should be seen as a potential key success factor for globally operating companies. Herewith, they should not forget to "think global, act local" (Interview III 2012: 5; Interview IV 2012: 4)!
Since all companies depend on their customers, it seems inevitable to listen to their suggestions. Within social media, the direct engagement is possible and companies can benefit enormously. As Buchanan (Interview III 2012: 4) argues, companies have to provide valuable content for customers instead of posting news about the weather. Otherwise they cannot expect their customers to share this content and distribute it further.
Within the survey conducted in this research, the SNS users in the BRIC countries were asked to give suggestions for the improvement of the SNS presences of BMW, adidas and NIVEA. The results are shown in the following graph (figure 48).

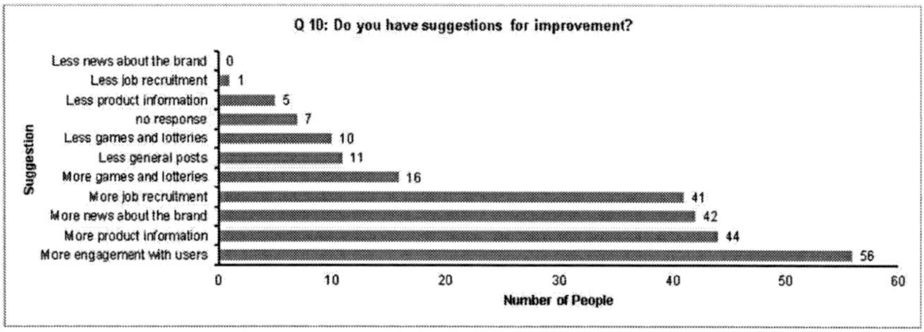

Figure 48: Suggestions for Improvement – BMW, adidas and NIVEA
Source: Own Illustration.

One striking result was that the users were not complaining about too many posts, but instead expressed their interest in more company contributions. The majority of users stated the desire of more direct engagement, as already outlined in figure 45. More product information, more news about the brand as well as more job recruitment were suggested as major points for improving the company SNS.

It can be concluded that in general BMW, adidas and NIVEA still don't provide enough information about their brands and products. All examined companies should think about monitoring their customers in a more specific way, in order to adapt and in the end improve their marketing approaches through more and better awareness. Recruiting processes via SNS should also constitute a key focus for companies. Nearly half of the survey participants suggested BMW, adidas and NIVEA to improve this aspect on their BRIC SNS.

People trust recommendations from their social networks to a great extent (chapter 2). The confidence in advice from others was ranked on the first place (Nielsen 2007). Since through weak ties information is being widely spread and distributed with an enormous speed, job vacancies at BMW, adidas and NIVEA could be shared with and by customers as well. This could lead to an increase of applicants for the companies and therefore imply greater possibilities to choose the best suiting employees. Moreover, at less cost they could reach even more potential applicants in less time around the world.

Social media has to be seen as more than just a channel to promote products. If companies want to be attractive, they have to provide content, which is desired and interesting to people who are potentially willing to share contents.

> [W]enn man diesen Netzwerkfaktor in einer guten Form hinbekommen möchte, muss man den Leuten etwas bieten, etwas was die Leute erstens interessiert und zweitens etwas, was die Leute bereit sind zu teilen. Ich muss einen Mechanismus entwickeln, der die Leute dazu bringt, den Inhalt zu teilen. Dann werde ich großen Erfolg haben (Interview III 2012: 4).

With further regard to the BRIC countries, the development of social media is seen as "great" (Interview I 2012: 8). The penetration of social networking is continuously increasing (Interview V 2012: 2; Interview I 2012: 2, 8).

Kopka (Interview IV 2012: 4) states that the time of mass media has been replaced by the time of the media mass, where everyone is representing a part of media. "Das war die Zeit der Massenmedien. Heute leben wir in der Zeit der Medienmassen. Jeder ist ein Stück weit selber Medium". For the first time, the direct engagement is possible. Therefore, "what is absolutely clear is that companies have to expand their presence on social networks" (Interview I 2012: 5- 8).

The subsequent chapter is summarizing the most valuable findings and concludes crucial aspects.

6 Conclusion: The Inevitability to Operate in Social Networks

The BRIC countries are gaining in importance. Social media usage in BRIC is steadily increasing. "The world of organizations is no longer defined by national boundaries" (Adler and Gundersen 2008: v).

> But who is the winner of this new world? Customers and good companies win - which, as a society, we have been trying to achieve since the industrial revolution. Good companies view negative feedback as an opportunity to act and adjust their products or services accordingly; bad companies view it as a nuisance or something they need to put an effort towards hiding. Social media is helping enable a truly connected world (Qualman 2011: 280).

With regard to the research question, which success factors are crucial for companies when implementing social media marketing in the most relevant SNS of the BRIC countries, the examination of BMW, adidas and NIVEA revealed valuable insights.

This research showed that it is not only important to be present in social networks with a global brand presence, but in addition with country pages designed to meet local language(s) and preferences. In order to adapt directly to the culture of a target group, traditions and cultural contexts have to be known, respected and applied. More than 50% of survey participants expressed the desire of a more localised appearance of the SNS of BMW, adidas and NIVEA. Moreover, companies have to be present and active within their SNS. In terms of these aspects, BMW serves as a good example, especially in Brazil, where it was evaluated especially well and outperformed NIVEA as well as adidas.

The quality of a company's commitment is particularly relevant. For users of the studied SNS, engagement was stated one of the most crucial aspects, ranked first as a suggestion for improvement. Moreover, 88% of respondents had the opinion that BMW, adidas and NIVEA could in general engage more. It should be focused more on quality instead of quantity. Customers should be monitored and it should be listened to their suggestions, in order to adapt in the best way -"first listen and monitor" (Interview I 2012: 6). "Ich glaube, jedes Unternehmen muss, und da bin ich wirklich bei jedem Unternehmen, mindestens "Monitoring" betreiben" (Interview IV 2012: 6-7). In accordance with the obtained knowledge from the target group, companies can directly adapt in the right way. Survey respondents encouraged content in the form of more news about the brand, more product information, and job postings. By answering to these suggestions, BMW, adidas and NIVEA could gain more clients, improve their reputation, and expect a positive impact on their revenue streams.

Social media is integrating more in our everyday lives and has become part of our lifestyle (Interview I 2012: 4; Interview III 2012: 2). "Wir stehen noch ganz am Anfang der Entwicklung und das wird auch in der Geschwindigkeit noch eine ganze Zeit so weitergehen" (Interview IV 2012: 3). In this new transparent world, companies can no longer hide (Qualman 2011: 280). Companies should be aware that by way of presence in social media they can co-determine the market directly and engage with customers.

BRIC countries already offer great potential for social media and the share of social media users is expected to increase significantly (Interview III 2012: 4-7; Interview II 2012: 2). As social media experts Schöllhammer (Interview I 2012: 3) and Buchanan (Interview III 2012: 6) stress: "...and if I don't use this networking, I will have a problem", because presence is inevitable: "Generell ist die Präsenz [in Social Media Sites; E.T.] ein Muss".

7 Future Perspectives

It is currently not predictable in which direction social media is going to develop in the longer term (Interview V 2012: 2). Since social media first came into being some years ago, "nobody knows how to behave in the right way. Everything is changing all the time" (Interview VI 2012: 3). Therefore, companies should always stay flexible and be aware of alterations, in order to adapt as early as possible. The increasing use of the microblogging site Sina Weibo, for example, is likely to leave other social media sites behind.

The growing economic relevance of social media is demonstrated by the recent Initial Public Offering (IPO) of Facebook in 2012. This shows that Facebook identified the potential of social media as a marketing source by selling space for advertisement on its network to companies directly.

If companies developed their own strategies by monitoring the customers' content, social media would likely increase as a valuable marketing and communication tool. The interaction with customers and the aspect of acknowledging different cultural contexts should hereby be emphasised (Weinfurter 2011).

Brazil, Russia, India and China are not the only emerging markets characterised by increasing social media exposure. South Africa, Mexico, Indonesia, Korea, Turkey or the Eastern European countries such as Poland, also characterized by a growing inflow of the foreign direct investments (OECD 2010), constitute other highly interesting targets for the development of company social media presences. In some views, South Africa has already become a part of the BRIC, expanding this terms to "the BRICS" and making the group even more euphonious (Hadas, E. 2011; Goldman Sachs 2003: 11). Companies have to cope with a global changing landscape -- but as Andy Warhol (1975: 111) stated: "They always say time changes things, but you actually have to change them yourself".

V. References

Absatzwirtschaft (2008). *Große Displayanzeigen verlieren gegenüber Suchmaschinenmarketing.* Retrieved 03/04/2012, from http://www.absatzwirtschaft.de/content/communication/news/grosse-displayanzeigen-verlieren-gegenueber-suchmaschinenmarketing;64522.

Acquisti, A., Gross, R. (2006). Imagined Communities: Awareness, Information Sharing, and Privacy on the Facebook. *Lecture Notes in Computer Sciences* 4258 (10), 36-58.

Adidas Group (2011). *Adidas Group. Annual Report 2011.* Retrieved 15/04/2012, from http://Adidas-group.corporate-publications.com/2011/gb/.

Adidas (2012). *Adidas.* Retrieved 15/04/2012, from http://www.Adidas.de/.

Adler, N. J., Gundersen, A. (2008). *International Dimensions of Organizational Behavior* (8th edition). Mason: Thomson South-Western.

Amine, L., Chao, M. & Arnold, M. (2005). Exploring the Practical Effects of Country of Origin, Animosity, and Price-Quality Issues: Two Case Studies of Taiwan and Acer in China. *Journal of International Marketing* 13 (2), 114-150.

Armstrong et al. (2009). *Marketing. An Introduction.* Harlow: Pearson Education Ltd.

Bächle, M. (2006). Aktuelles Schlagwort Social Software. *Informatik Spektrum* 29 (2), 121-124.

Bilkey, B., Nes, E. (1982). Country-of-Origin Effects on Product Evaluations. *Journal of International Business Studies* 13 (2), 89-99.

Blog VK (2008). *Рост ВКонтакте Pavel Durov.* Retrieved 10/04/2012, from http://vk.com/blog?act=s&nid=88.

BMW Group (2010). *BMW Group. Annual Report 2012.* Retrieved 15/04/2012, from http://www.bmwgroup.com/bmwgroup_prod/e/0_0_www_bmwgroup_com/investor_relations/finanzberichte/_pdf/BMW_Group_AR2010.pdf.

BMW Group (2012). *BMW Group. Official Website.* Retrieved 15/04/2012, from http://www.bmwgroup.com/bmwgroup_prod/e/nav/index.html?http://www.bmwgroup.com/bmwgroup_prod/e/0_0_www_bmwgroup_com/home/home.html.

Borodina, S., Shvyrkov, O. (2010). *Investing in BRIC countries. Evaluating Risk and Governance in Brazil, Russia, India & China.* New York: McGraw-Hill.

Boyd, D., Ellison, N.B. (2008). Social Network Sites: Definition, History, and Scholarship. *Journal of Computer-Mediated Communication* 13 (1), 210-230.

Burt, R. S. (1992). *Structural Holes.The Social Structure of Competition.* Harvard: Harvard University Press.

Burt, R. S. (2004). Structural Holes and Good Ideas. *American Journal of Sociology* 110 (2), 349-399.

BVDW. (2011). *Umfrage zur Veränderung des Social-Media-Budgets in Unternehmen.* Retrieved 04/04/2012, from Statista database http://de.statista.com/statistik/daten/studie/214152/umfrage/umfrage-zur-entwicklung-des-social-media-budgets-in-unternehmen/.

Clifton, R. and Maughan, E. (2000). *The Future of Brands. Twenty-five visions.* London: MACMILLAN Press Ltd.

Durkheim, É. (1893). *De la division du travail social.* Québec: L'Université du Québec.

eBiz MBA (2012). *The 15 Most Popular Social Networking Sites*. Retrieved 09/04/2012, from http://www.ebizmba.com/articles/social-networking-websites.

Endeshaw, A. (2004). Internet Regulation in China: The Never Ending-Ending Cat and Mouse Game1. *Information & Communications Technology Law* 13 (1), 41-57.

Evans, J. (1994). Aristotle on Politics. *The Classical Review* 44 (2), 300-302.

Facebook (2012). *Facebook Newsroom. Fact Sheet*. Retrieved 09/04/2012, from http://newsroom.fb.com/content/default.aspx?NewsAreaId=22.

flickr fredcavazza (2008). *Social Media Landscape*. Retrieved 11/04/2012, from http://www.flickr.com/photos/fredcavazza/2564571564/.

Forbes (2011). *Facebook Surpasses Orkut. Owned by Google. In Numbers of Users in Brazil.* Retrieved 09/04/2012, from http://www.forbes.com/sites/ricardogeromel/2011/09/14/facebook-surpasses-orkut-owned-by-google-in-numbers-of-users-in-brazil/.

Fu, Z., Wu, J. (2011). *RDURP '11 Proceedings of the 2011 ACM Symposium on The Role of Design in UbiComp Research & Practice*. New York: ACM.

globeone (2011). *BRIC Branding Survey*. Retrieved 15/04/2012, from http://www.slideshare.net/globeone_/bric-branding-survey-the-perception-of-german-brands-in-the-worlds.

Goldkorn, J. (2011). *TechCrunch. Renren: Big but not the Facebook of China*. Retrieved 10/04/2012, from http://techcrunch.com/2011/05/03/renren-big-but-not-the-facebook-of-china/.

Goldman Sachs (2003). *Dreaming with BRICs. The Path to 2050*. Retrieved 06/04/2012, from http://www.goldmansachs.com/our-thinking/brics/brics-reports-pdfs/brics-dream.pdf.

Goldman Sachs (2011). A Progress Report on the Builduing of the BRICs. *BRICs Monthly* 11 (7), 1-4.

Grabher, G., Maintz, J. (2007). Learning in Personal Networks: Collaborative Knowledge Production in Virtual Forums. In H. Hof and U. Wengenroth (eds.) *Innovationsforschung* (187-201). Hamburg: LIT Verlag.

Granovetter, M. S. (1973). The Strength of Weak Ties. *American Journal of Sociology* 78 (6), 1360-1380.

Hadas, E. (2011). *Breakingviews. Agenda setting financial insight*. Retrieved 21/04/2012, from http://www.breakingviews.com/bric-success-shows-the-power-of-a-good-idea/1617696.article.

Harvey, C. R. (1994). *Predictable Risk and Returns in Emerging Markets*. Retrieved 05/04/2012, from http://www.nber.org/papers/w4621.pdf.

Hettler, U. (2010). *Social Media Marketing. Marketing mit Blogs, Sozialen Netzwerken und weiteren Anwendungen des Web 2.0*. München: Oldenbourg.

Hofstede, G. (2001). *Culture's Consequences. Comparing Values, Behaviors, Institutions and Organizations across Nations* (2nd edition). Thousand Oaks: Sage.

Internet World Stats (2011). *World Internet Users and Population Stats*. Retrieved 09/04/2012, from http://www.internetworldstats.com/stats.htm.

IT Times (2012). *Sina profitiert vom Microblogging-Boom. Sina Weibo zählt 300 Millionen Nutzer*. Retrieved 11/04/2012, from http://www.it-times.de/news/hintergrundbericht/datum/2012/02/29/sina-profitiert-vom-microblogging-boom-sina-weibo-zaehlt-300-millionen-nutzer/.

Katz, J. (2012). *Competing for Global Dominance. Survival in a Changing World.* Cupertino: superstarpress.

Kekic, L. (2009). The Global Economic Crisis and FDI Flows to Emerging Markets. *Columbia FDI Perspectives* 15 (10), 1-5.

Kogut, B., Zander, U. (1992). Knowledge Of The Firm and The Evolutionary Theory Of The Multinational Corporation. *Journal of International Business Studies* 24 (4), 625-645.

Levin, D. Z., Cross, R. (2004). The Strength of Weak Ties You Can Trust: The Mediating Role of Trust in Effective Knowledge Transfer. *Management Science* 50 (11), 1477-1490.

Li, C., Bernoff, J. (2008). *Groundswell. Winning in a World Transformed by Social Technologies*. Boston: Harvard Business Press.

Lukoff, K. (2011a). *Mashable Business. What Makes China's Top 4 Social Networks Tick?* Retrieved 11/04/2012, from http://mashable.com/2011/03/18/china-top-social-network/.

Lukoff, K. (2011b). *TechRice. China's Top 15 Social Networks.* Retrieved 10/04/2012, from http://techrice.com/2011/03/08/chinas-top-15-social-networks/.

Madia, S., Borgese, P. (2010). *The Social Media Survival Guide. Everything You Need to Know to Grow Your Business Expotentially with Social Media.* New Jersey: Full Court Press.

Magnaglobal (2012). *Online-Werbung-Statista Dossier 2012.* Retrieved 03/04/2011, from Statista database http://de.statista.com/statistik/daten/studie/185637/umfrage/Prognose-der-Entwicklung-der-Ausgaben-für-Online-Werbung-weltweit/.

Malhotra, N., Birks, D. (2006). *Marketing Research. An Applied Approach* (3rd edition). Essex: Pearson Education.

Malhotra, N. K. (2007). *Marketing Research. An Applied Orientation* (5th edition). Upper Saddle River: Pearson Education.

Mangold, W., Faulds, D. (2009). Social Media: The New Hybrid Element of The Promotion Mix. *Business Horizons* 52 (4), 357-365.

Marr, J., Reynard, C. (2010). *Investing in Emerging Markets. The BRIC Economies and Beyond.* Chichester: Wiley and Sons, Ltd.

Maslow, A. (1970). *Motivation and Personality.* New York: Harper & Row.

McQuarrie, E. F. (2006). *The Market Research Toolbox. A Concise Guide for Beginners* (2nd edition). Thousand Oaks: Sage.

Meckl, R. (2010). *Internationales Management* (2nd edition). München: Franz Vahlen.

Meffert, H., Burmann, C. & Kirchgeorg, M. (2008). *Marketing. Grundlagen marktorientierter Unternehmensführung* (11th edition). Wiesbaden: Gabler.

Milgram, S. (1969). The Small-World Problem. *Psychology Today* 1 (1), 61-67.

Miller, H. (2010). *Culture and Work Style in the BRIC countries. Research Summary.* Retrieved 20/11/2011, from http://www.hermanmiller.com/MarketFacingTech/hmc/research/research_summaries/assets/wp_BRIC_Countries.pdf.

Millward Brown Optimor (2011). *Erwartungen von Unternehmen im Social Web.* Retrieved 03/04/2012, from Statista database http://de.statista.com/statistik/daten/studie/177513/umfrage/die-wertvollsten-chinesische-marken.

Mühlenbeck, F., Skibicki, K. (2007). *Community Marketing Management. Wie man Online-Communities im Internet-Zeitalter des Web 2.0 zum Erfolg führt.* Köln: Brain Injection.

Mühlenbeck, F., Skibicki, K. (2010). *Die TOP100 Strategie für Social Media Marketing. 100 Praxis-Tipps zur Positionierung Ihrer Marke und zum Verkauf Ihrer Produkte mit Facebook, YouTube, Twitter und Co.* Köln: Brain Injection.

Nickels, W. G., McHugh, J. & McHugh, S. (2008). *Understanding Business* (8th edition). New York: McGraw-Hill.

Nielsen (2007). *Word-of-Mouth. The Most Powerful Selling Tool: Nielsen Global Survey.* Retrieved 04/04/2012, from http://www.nielsen.com/us/en/insights/press-room/2007/Word-of-Mouth_the_Most_Powerful_Selling_Tool__Nielsen_Global_Survey.html.

NIVEA (2010). *nivea. Annual Report 2012.* Retrieved 15/04/2012, from http://www.annualreport2010.beiersdorf.com/en/home/64-100-jahre-nivea.html.

NIVEA (2012). *nivea.* Retrieved 15/04/2012, from http://www.nivea.de/.

OECD (2010). *Foreign Direct Investment: Main Aggregates.* Retrieved 23/04/2012, from OECD International Direct Investment Statistics database http://stats.oecd.org/BrandedView.aspx?oecd_bv_id=idi-data-en&doi=data-00338-en#.

Offbeat China (2011). *Profiling China's Top 5 Social Networks - China Social Media 1.* Retrieved 11/04/2012, from http://offbeatchina.com/profiling-china%E2%80%99s-top-social-media-1-%E2%80%93-sns-social-networking-sites.

O'Reilly, T. (2006). *O'Reilly Radar.* Retrieved 23/03/2012, from http://radar.oreilly.com/2006/12/web-20-compact-definition-tryi.html.

Parekh, R. (2011). *Global Ad Spending to Grow only 4,2%.* Retrieved 07/04/2012, from http://adage.com/article/mediaworks/global-ad-spending-grow-4-2/226903/.

PricewaterhouseCoopers (2011). *Economic Views Global.* Retrieved 10/04/2011, from http://www.pwc.com/et_EE/EE/publications/assets/pub/economic-views-global-december-2011.pdf.

PricewaterhouseCoopers (2012). *The World in 2050.* Retrieved 06/04/2011, from http://www.pwc.com/en_GX/gx/world-2050/pdf/world-in-2050-jan-2011.pdf.

PSFK (2012). *Every 60 Seconds in China.* Retrieved 10/04/2012 from http://www.psfk.com/2012/01/internet-stats-china.html.

Qualman, E. (2011). *Socialnomics. How Social Media Transforms the Way We Live and Do Business.* New Jersey: John Wiley & Sons, Inc.

Renren (2012). *The Leading Real Name SNS in China.* Retrieved 11/04/2012, from http://renren-inc.com/en/.

Schiller, D. (2001). *Das Netz verkommt zum Kiosk.* Retrieved 10/03/2012, from http://www.zeit.de/2001/12/Das_Netz_verkommt_zum_Kiosk.

Schwarz, T. (2008). *Erfolgreiches Online Marketing. Schritt für Schritt zum Ziel.* München: Haufe.

Sina Weibo (2011). *Annual Report 2011.* Retrieved 10/04/2012, from http://tech.sina.com.cn/i/2010-11-16/10314870771.shtml.

Smith, A. (1964). Adam Smith's Two Views on the Division of Labour. *Economica* 31 (121), 23-32.

State Council Information Office of the People's Republic of China (2010). *The Internet in China.* Retrieved 10/04/2012, from http://www.scio.gov.cn/zxbd/wz/201006/t667385.htm.

Stelzner, M. (2010). *How Marketers Are Using Social Media To Grow Their Businesses. Social Media Marketing Report.* Retrieved 19/11/2011, from Statista database http://de.statista.com/statistik/daten/studie/214152/umfrage/umfrage-zur-entwicklung-des-social-media-budgets-in-unternehmen/.

Swann, C., Hadas, E. (2011). *BRIC Power.* Retrieved 13/04/2012, from http://www.nytimes.com/2011/11/29/business/global/chinas-advantage-in-helping-europe.html.

Szugat, M., Gewehr, J. & Lochmann, C. (2006). *Social Software. Blogs, Wikis & Co.* Frankfurt am Main: Entwickler Press.

Toffler Associates (2012). *40 for the next 40. A Sampling of the drivers of change that will shape our world between now and 2050.* Retrieved 01/03/2012, from http://www.toffler.com/docs/40%20for%20the%20Next%2040%20101011%20FINAL.pdf.

Travers, J.. Milgram, S. (1969). An Experimantal Study of the Small World Problem. *Sociometry* 32 (4), 425-443.

United Nations (2010). *World Population Prospects.* Retrieved 21/04/2012, from http://esa.un.org/unpd/wpp/index.htm.

United States Securities and Exchange Commission (2011). *Registration Statement Facebok Inc.* Retrieved 09/04/2012, from http://sec.gov/Archives/edgar/data/1326801/000119312512034517/d287954ds1.htm.

Van Agtmael, A. (2007). *The Emerging Markets Century. How a New Breed of World-Class Companies Is Overtaking the World.* New York: Free Press.

Vital World Consulting (2009). *Emerging Markets Definition and World Market Segments.* Retrieved 05/04/2012, from http://www.vitalwaveconsulting.com/pdf/Emerging%20Markets%20Definition%20and%20World%20Market%20Groups.pdf.

VKontakte (2012). *About VK.* Retrieved 10/04/2012, from http://vk.com/help.php?page=about.

Weinfurter, P. (2011). *Social Media ohne Facebook. Potentiale des Social Webs in China.* Retrieved 22/04/2012, from http://allfacebook.de/allgemeines/social-media-ohne-facebook-potentiale-des-social-webs-in-china-whitepaper.

Yu, L., Asur, S. & Huberman, B. (2011). *What Trends in Chinese Social Media.* Retrieved 10/04/2012, from http://www.hpl.hp.com/research/scl/papers/chinatrends/china_trends.pdf.

Zerfass et al. (2011). *European Communication Monitor.* Retrieved 11/04/2012, from http://www.zerfass.de/ecm/ECM2011-Results-ChartVersion.pdf.

VI. Appendix

VII. List of Interview Partners

Expert Interview Partners
Social Media/ Marketing/ Consultancy

Interview I: Participant: Ruth Schöllhammer
Managing Director
Consultancy and Project Management Social Media

Interview II: Participant: Christian Offer
Consultant
OSCAR GmbH/ OFW Student Consulting and Research

Interview III: Participant: Alex Buchanan
Managing Director
BRS Social Media Marketing UG

Interview IV: Participant: Marc-Sven Kopka
VP Corporate Communication
XING AG

Interview V: Participant: Dr. Alexandra Wöllenstein
Director – Strategy and Conception
Stuewe Management Consulting GmbH

Interview VI: Participant: Jorge Junior
Marketing Analyst
BMW Group Brazil

VIII. Interview Guideline

Expert Interview
Main Threat: Social Media Marketing in BRIC Countries

1. **General information about the interviewee**
- Age.
- How long have you been active in the field of social media and what is your experience?
- What is your current position?

2. **Development of Social Media**
- Why do you think do people use social media?
- What do you think about the development of social media in general? Do you think social media will grow further with the same speed? Where do you see the endpoint of social media?
- For which aspects do you think social media could be used and in which direction do you think social media is going to develop (socializing, business etc.)?
- Where do you see chances, challenges and limits of social media for global German companies e.g. BMW, adidas, NIVEA?
- Granovetter, an American sociologist, stresses in his study "the strength of weak ties" that within social networks the flow of information is increased through the existence of weak ties.What are the main success factors for a global company to use these weak ties successfully?

3. **Social Media Marketing**
- What are the main aspects of social media which differentiate this marketing channel from others such as TV, radio, newspapers, etc.?
- Which criteria are crucial when measuring success for companies when entering social networks for marketing purposes (likes, comments, etc.)
- When entering social networks as a global company, which main aspects have to be considered?
- Do you think the social media activity of a global brand should be adapted to different countries (e.g. having different fan pages for different countries, in order to adapt to culture, or one page)?
- What are the key success factors for local adaption in social media (national models, traditions, use of local language, etc.)?

4. **Social Media Marketing in BRIC Countries**
- Do you think it is inevitable to enter social media networks as a marketing strategy when entering foreign markets?
- For which companies do you think is it most important to be active in social networks?

- Imagine the following scenario: You are the social media marketing officer of a global German brand which wants to improve its social media activity in the networks of the BRIC Countries (Brazil, Russia, India, China).
    - Which steps would you take?
    - What is the main criterion to consider?
    - What do you think about the future development of social media marketing in the BRIC Countries?

5. Prospect and Review

- Do you have any questions from your side or further remarks?

IX. Interview I

Interview I
Date: 12.03.2012, 18.20h – 19.30h
Participant: Ruth Schöllhammer

I. General information about the interviewee

Trost: May I ask you for your age?

Schöllhammer: *Yes, I'm 48.*

Trost: How long have you been active in the field of social media and what is your experience?

Schöllhammer: *In 2007, I started to work independently on the topic WEB 2.0 and started to make my own study: The Web 2.0 typology. The reason why I conducted this study was because I wanted to know why people are active in this so called "Web 2.0" and not how long etc.*
So, we created a real first typology and found out that people reading newspapers, e.g. the magazine chip, are thinking differently as people active in social media, as an example, active in a forum.
In 1996, I was the first online editor at "Werben und Verkaufen". So it was a smooth transition concerning social media.

Trost: What is your current position?

Schöllhammer: *Since 2007, I am self-employed in consultancy and project management in social media, giving workshops and seminars in this field and moreover teaching in several universities.*

II. Development of Social Media

Trost: Why do you think people are using social media?

Schöllhammer: *Why are people talking? Social media is mainly about generating content. And the main aspect of social media is to have conversations and the dialogue between people. So, the question is why people are talking. And what we can find out or rather found out is that there are the so called "Kommunikationstreiber", drivers for communication.*
From my point of view, I would define these drivers as the following:
First of all it's about proximity. People like to talk about what's going on around them, in their direct neighbourhood etc. Secondly, it's about giving advice. "Help, I am pregnant!" In order to get immediate reactions, people want to be active in social networks. Furthermore, identity and values are important, as an example the case of IngDiBa how vegetari-

ans are differentiating themselves from vegans. And then it's also about hobbies. These are the key drivers or motivation for communication, in order to inform others and myself and share information. There is a lot of rubbish and nonsense around us going on in this virtual world, which we also experience in our everyday life. But nevertheless, we need this as a kind of social kit, this is social communication. And therefore we use these social networks such as Facebook, etc. This represents for me social networking. Drivers for this kind of networking are: social communication, the desire to socialise and talk, stand with other people in contact, having dialogues and then the corresponding motives.

If we talk about social media in general, this is even more than just social networking. Social media is Wikipedia, Twitter, blogs, YouTube, content sharing, slide sharing, forums and so on and so on. But I always have to consider the different drivers and motivation people have.

Trost: Ok and what do you think about the development of social media in general? Do you think social media will grow further with the same speed? Where do you see the endpoint of social media?

Schöllhammer: *The penetration of social media and especially of social networking is increasing enormously.*
Well, I don't know where we will reach an endpoint. It varies from country to country. I also think that this is a cultural aspect. So, for example German people are critical in terms of communication. We, as Germans totally distinguish between our private life and our profession; we have a strong separation in this field. "What happens, if my boss can read about my personal life?" This aspect is not the case in other cultures, also not in the BRIC countries.
The access to social media and therefore to social networks mainly depends on the access of technology. Technology have to be available to people and it need to be ensured that they have access in the form of Internet connection, availability of the networks, tools, etc.
The development is limited by the access of technique and not by culture.

Trost: For which aspects do you think social media could be used and in which direction do you think social media is going to develop (socializing, business etc.)?

Schöllhammer: *It's about socializing, yes. Mainly it's about dialogue, the dialogue between people and furthermore about the aspect of networking, being connected and finding the connection to others. From my perspective, not the view of a user but instead, more from the view of a company, the main criterion for success is the USP. Now, through social media, the aspect of networking was added and if I don't use this networking, I will have a problem. Networking is not only the dialogue and the conversation with my customer, but also with other stakeholders, its maintaining contacts with employees and establishing contacts with universities, etc.*
Social media mainly has to do something with the whole corporate culture. I need this networking effect in my company, in my corporate culture, so that my employees can speak

with other stakeholders on the same platform. In Germany, this is still a problem and it's different in other countries, also in the BRIC ones.
Concerning businesses and the development of social media, more and more people are connected to social networks as a company.
In previous times you had to be on the "Yellow Pages" to be found, then on Google and now the presence in social networks like Facebook is required to be found. So, without any question, you have to be present nowadays in social media and active in social networks. The only question is how do I present myself?
As an example, asking my students if they are friends with some famous brands in social networks, the answer often is no, but in the end it turns out that they are friends with L'Oreal, adidas or Coca Cola. This is just not realised any more as advertisement. It has become part of our lifestyle. And this exactly is the aim of companies; they have to become a part of our lifestyle. And here, social networks like Facebook & Co. are just part of this new lifestyle.

Trost: Where do you see chances, challenges and limits of social media for global German companies, e.g. BMW, adidas, NIVEA?

Schöllhammer: *It is clear, if I talk about social networking, then I just can have this conversation directly on site. It can't be centralised. Therefore, the challenge is to be part of this lifestyle. And to become part of the lifestyle, I have to enter into a discussion with people. And this discussion needs to have different triggers as I already mentioned before.*
Well, it's clear, that companies such as BMW, etc. wants to get rid of information, but this information needs to be relevant. And to ensure this relevance, I need people on site, local people with inside information. Humour is of major importance. Humour for example in Brazil or India is totally different then here. The different cultures have to be considered.

Trost: *Granovetter, an American sociologist, stresses in his study "the strength of weak ties" that within social networks, the flow of information is increased through the existence of weak ties.*
What are the main success factors for a global company to use these weak ties successfully?

Schöllhammer: *Well, first of all, I totally agree with the existence of weak ties in social networks. It can be compared directly with our real life: If we go to an event, concert, etc., we always meet the same people. These are not your real friends; they just belong to your extended friends. And normally you meet these people maybe two to three times a year. Now, here in social media you always have these weak ties around you, so you have a totally different range, which is much larger than ever before.*
Companies are absolutely using these weak ties, but it always depends on the department how these ties are used.
For example in marketing they want to improve its level of awareness. So, therefore I need money. This is not only possible just through these weak ties. I need to make advertisement and buy apps, etc.

If we talk about image, building up confidence and trust, then social networks and these weak ties directly help me. I need to have a structural plan, credibility and authenticity. If we talk about the topic of relevance and first choice, then I need histories and can do specific sale activities.
So, how I use these weak ties, it always depends on the objective of the department.
First of all, I always need awareness, then a huge range, then image, a kind of relevant set and then I reach first choice. These 4 points are crucial. These points I always need. Then, I have to think of the platform I want to use and about my content, etc. And, in my point of view, this is the aspect where companies are still weak, doesn't matter if they are small or big. They have to know their goals, their structural plan, have to consider the cultural aspects for example humour of the people. What's the humour of people and how can we connect this humour with our strategies? Another question companies have to ask themselves is how to realise image and how to achieve greater proximity and then, what they have and want to post next. These are issues companies have to improve for sure.

III. Social Media Marketing

Trost: What are the main aspects of social media which differ this marketing channel from others such as TV, radio, newspapers, etc.?

Schöllhammer: *First, there is monitoring and then I want to start talking with people, and I can't talk with people via TV. I need engagement and have to answer the question what I exactly want from my target group except of buying my product. What else can they do for me? Do I want that my customers recommend something for me or upload pictures or write experience reports? There are totally different ways of engagement. First, I have to think what I want. And this question is definitely asked by not enough companies at the moment.*
Through the present of social media, it's the first time that people are working for me directly. I have a huge range and user generated content. I also could have asked for experience reports via traditional media in the past, but the probability to receive something back was not too high.
Tchibo as an example has a so called "idea platform". Here, users are generating product ideas. Suddenly, the marketing department and the department for product development have to work together. This networking among departments has to be considered and is reflected by social networks.
And this has to be the case in companies as well. So, first of all companies should be connected in its corporate culture and then starting to be connected in their social media strategy. A social media department seems to be inevitable.

Trost: Which criteria are crucial when measuring success for companies, entering social networks as a marketing strategy (likes, comments, etc.)?

Schöllhammer: *Social media marketing has to be broken down, in order to have success. It always depends on the goals. I can use specific measures and that's great. If I post about product information and my goal is to increase brand awareness, then I can look at the* *likes. If I for example talk about a new employee, I should rather look at the content of comments. It always depends on my objectives and has to be broken down.*

Trost: When entering social networks as a global company, which main aspects have to be considered?

Schöllhammer: *First listen and monitor. That's crucial in my opinion. I have to get an overview of what's going on in all social networks and not just look for one dimension. They are all connected, Facebook, Twitter, blogs, etc. I have to consider which people to target and search where I can reach them in the best way, where they are active and what they are doing.*
Then, I have to define user groups. I should have set up my guidelines in the headquarter before to clarify who will be responsible for certain tasks, how to react to complaints, etc. Then, I have to interpret these issues and apply them to the new culture I am entering. I have to work in a team to get better results.

Trost: Do you think the social media activity of a global brand should be adapted to different countries (e.g. having different fan pages for different countries, in order to adapt to culture, or one page)?

Schöllhammer: *I wouldn't think exclusively, but I think it's relevant to have different pages, in order to react directly with local people. But nevertheless, I also think that a general page for each brand is necessary too. Here, I just focus on different people.*

Trost: What are the key success factors for local adaption in social media (national models, traditions, use of local language etc.)?

Schöllhammer: *I have to think about culture. I probably have another humour, if I think for example about bikinis in Brazil and in Germany. We have to clarify these intercultural aspects and how to interpret them in a uniform way.*
We have to know which topics are important for which countries and cultures, in order to adapt my product information in the best way. These things have to be clarified at first.

IV. Social Media Marketing in BRIC countries

Trost: Do you think it's inevitable to enter social media networks as a marketing strategy when entering foreign country markets?

Schöllhammer: *Yes, because I want to stay in contact with people and want to have talks.*

Trost: For which companies do you think it's the most important to be active in social networks?

Schöllhammer: *It always depends on the company and on the objective I have as a company, where I am active or what I am doing.*
I am convinced that if people change from Google as a starting page to Facebook, which at the moment is 50/50, I have to be present in social networks. It doesn't matter in which way. What is absolutely clear is that companies have to expand their presence on social networks. About 50 % use Facebook as a starting page and don't want to leave this network anymore, and then, I have to start my campaigns in the corresponding social networks. It's like with Google. If people don't find me on Google, then I don't exist.

Trost: Now, imagine the following scenario: You are the social media marketing officer of a global German brand who wants to improve its social media activity in the networks of the BRIC countries (Brazil, Russia, India, China). Which steps would you take?

Schöllhammer: *Monitoring. Which platforms are relevant for me? Which topics are being discussed in these networks? I have to know about what people are talking!*

Trost: What is the main criterion to consider?

Schöllhammer: *Well, it always depends on the objective. But it's important that I cooperate with people directly and active in these networks. I need to know the crucial aspects to consider when entering other countries and cultures. I have to enter these communities and ask the people directly. I have to involve people directly in my social media activities. I can adapt and in this way, I am increasing my success.*

Trost: What do you think about the future development of social media marketing in the BRIC countries?

Schöllhammer: *Great!! As soon as the technical aspects will be realised, more gadgets, more tools, etc., the BRIC countries are going to improve even more. In social media just basic needs of the people are satisfied.*

V. Prospect and Review

Trost: Do you have any questions from your side or further remarks?

Schöllhammer: *No questions, thanks. I'm just interested in your thesis and would like to read it afterwards, if possible.*

Trost: No problem at all and thank you very much for your time.

X. Interview II

Interview II
Date: 14.03.2012, 17.00h – 17.35h
Participant: Christian Offer

I. General information about the interviewee

Trost: How old are you?

Offer: *Ich bin 28 Jahre alt.*

Trost: How long have you been active in the field of social media and what is your experience?

Offer: *Also aktiv im Social Media-Bereich bin ich seit ungefähr 5 Jahren und habe dort nur positive Erfahrungen gemacht, vor allem, um Kontakt zu halten. Und natürlich können hier auch viele Informationen generiert werden.*

Trost: What is your current position?

Offer: *Ich bin derzeit Projektmitarbeiter bei der studentischen Unternehmensberatung Oscar und betreue dort ein internes Projekt. Darin haben meine Projektpartnerin und ich einen Workshop zum Thema Social Media und Krisenmanagement mit Social Media auf dem World Business Dialogue durchgeführt.*

Trost: Können Sie mir genaueres zu dem Social Media-Projekt sagen? Was genau hatte es damit auf sich?

Offer: *Der Workshop lief unter dem Namen "DO and DONT'S for Companies in Social Media". Darin ging es darum aufzuzeigen, wie sich ein Unternehmen verhalten soll, wenn negative Kritik in den von ihnen betriebenen Social Media-Kanälen aufkommt. Dies haben wir anhand einer Fallstudie untersucht. Die Teilnehmer sollten lernen, was von Seiten eines Unternehmens wichtig ist, um einem sogenannten "Shitstorm" zuvorzukommen. Das Projekt ist sehr gut gelaufen und alle Teilnehmer waren am Ende sehr begeistert.*

II. Development of Social Media

Trost: Why do you think people are using social media?

Offer: *Grundsätzlich um sich zu vernetzen und um zu kommunizieren. Das ist der grundlegende Aspekt, würde ich sagen.*

Trost: What do you think about the development of social media in general? Do you think social media will grow further with the same speed? Where do you see the endpoint of social media?

Offer: *Grundsätzlich denke ich, dass sich die Nutzung von Social Media-Plattformen noch ausweiten wird. Nicht nur privat, sondern auch, dass immer mehr und mehr Unternehmen in Social Media eintreten werden, weil es meiner Meinung nach auch ein Zukunftsmarkt ist. Wenn man zum Beispiel das Thema F-Commerce betrachtet, was Facebook forciert: Man bekommt dort Credits mit denen man kaufen und verkaufen kann. Ob dies ein Erfolg wird, wird uns wohl nur die Zukunft zeigen können.*
Allerdings sind jetzt schon so viele Privatleute in sozialen Netzwerken wie Facebook aktiv, dass meiner Meinung nach eine Sättigung eintreten wird und somit die Nutzungszeit stagnieren oder sich sogar verringern wird. Das hat uns auch schon das Beispiel StudiVZ gezeigt, auch wenn dort eher eine Abwanderung zu Facebook zu verzeichnen war. Ich kenne das auch von Freunden. Es wird teilweise so viel unnötiger Content gepostet, dass man am Ende einfach nur noch genervt ist.

Trost: For which aspects do you think social media could be used and in which direction do you think social media is going to develop (socializing, business, etc.)?

Offer: *Im Bereich Business gehe ich davon aus, dass nach und nach fast alle Unternehmen in die sozialen Netzwerke eintreten werden. Hier wird die Möglichkeit geboten Recruiting zu praktizieren und relativ schnell eine große Masse anzusprechen. Zudem wird das F-Commerce, was ich zuvor bereits angesprochen habe, mit Sicherheit auch noch weiter in den Fokus kommen.*

Trost: Where do you see chances, challenges and limits of social media for global German companies, e.g. BMW, adidas, NIVEA?

Offer: *Grundsätzlich denke ich, dass es für jedes Unternehmen sinnvoll sein kann in Social Media einzutreten, sie müssen sich allerdings im Vorfeld Gedanken über die richtige Strategie machen. Sie sollten es nicht nur machen, weil andere Unternehmen im Social Media aktiv sind. Ein Unternehmen sollte im Vorfeld eine eigene, "customised" Strategie ausarbeiten, die dann umgesetzt wird. Ansonsten sollten Unternehmen die Finger davon lassen. Social Media kann ebenso den Markteintritt für neue Märkte unterstützen.*

Trost: Granovetter, an American sociologist, stresses in his study "the strength of weak ties", that within social networks, the flow of information is increased through the existence of weak ties. What are the main success factors for a global company to use these weak ties successfully?

Offer: *Ja, die Weak Ties sind wirklich wichtig. In den sozialen Netzwerken nennen sich viele Kontakte Freunde, auch wenn es nur Bekannte oder Bekannte von Bekannten sind.*

Ich denke, dass die Unternehmen in diesem Bereich auf die Leute zugehen und stets interessanten Content anbieten müssen, um die Leute für sich zu gewinnen. Somit haben sie die Möglichkeit, eine breite Masse an Leuten schnell für sich zu gewinnen, was auch durch die große Masse an Weak Ties unterstützt wird.

III. Social Media Marketing

Trost: What are the main aspects of social media which differ this marketing channel from others such as TV, radio, newspapers, etc.?

Offer: *Einmal natürlich ist es eine Kostenfrage. Die Kosten in Social Media sind weitaus geringer als beispielsweise für Fernseh- oder Radiowerbung. Zudem natürlich auch die Geschwindigkeit und die Häufigkeit, mit der man seine Nachricht verbreiten kann.*

Trost: Which criteria are crucial when measuring success for companies, entering social networks as a marketing strategy (likes, comments etc.)?

Offer: *Also es geht natürlich darum zu schauen, wie viele Fans ein Unternehmen hat, wie häufig ein Post des Unternehmens "geliked" wird, und über längere Dauer zu sehen, wie das Unternehmen sich um seine Fans kümmert. Ob es negative oder positive Posts auf ihrer Seite bekommt; wie häufig auf Posts geantwortet wird und wie lange für eine Antwort von Seiten des Unternehmens gebraucht wird. Das ist ein enorm wichtiger Faktor im Bereich Social Media, egal ob es sich nun um einen positiven oder negativen Post handelt. Erhalten die Fans keine Antwort oder dauert es zu lange, werden sie nicht lange als Fan gehalten werden können, da sie auf Dauer keinen Sinn darin sehen, etwas zu posten.*

Trost: When entering social networks as a global company, which main aspects have to be considered?

Offer: *Der erste Schritt besteht, wie schon erwähnt, in der Ausarbeitung einer Strategie. Dann müssen die Unternehmen sich genau überlegen, welchen Content es bieten wollen, und diesen in die strategischen Ziele des Unternehmens einbauen. Danach muss sie ins Unternehme integriert werden, das heißt, die Strategie muss ins Unternehmen gebracht werden und die Mitarbeiter mit ins Boot geholt werden. Also muss Akzeptanz für das Projekt geschaffen werden. Das bedeutet, dass die Mitarbeiter motiviert werden müssen, das Vorhaben zu unterstützen und dem Unternehmen den Rücken zu stärken, falls negative Kommentare aufkommen. Viele Mitarbeiter sind mit Sicherheit bereits schon privat in Social Media aktiv und kennen sich teilweise vielleicht sogar besser damit aus als die Entscheidungsträger des Unternehmens. Als letzten Punkt müssen Kontrollinstrumente geschaffen werden, um den Erfolg der Unternehmensbemühungen messen zu können. Grundsätzlich ist ein Account in den sozialen Netzwerken wie Facebook zum Beispiel kostenlos, allerdings muss das Unternehmen auch hier ein bestimmtes Budget und Ressourcen zur Verfügung stellen. Es muss immer frischen und interessanten Content liefern. Um dies garantieren zu können, muss von Seiten des Unternehmens investiert werden. Damit das Unternehmen den Erfolg* *der Investitionen kontrollieren kann, müssen also Instrumente erarbeitet werden, mit denen der Erfolg der Investitionen berechnet werden kann. Die Wichtigkeit dieser Punkte belegten auch die Ergebnisse unseres Workshops.*

Trost: Do you think the social media activity of a global brand should be adapted to different countries (e.g. having different fan pages for different countries, in order to adapt to culture, or one page)?

Offer: *Es ist meiner Meinung nach sinnvoll, wenn ein Unternehmen mit seiner Social Media-Präsenz auf den kulturellen Hintergrund des jeweiligen Landes eingehen kann.*

Trost: What are the key success factors for local adaption in social media (national models, traditions, use of local language, etc.)?

Offer: *Ich würde den Fokus auf die Bedürfnisse der Bevölkerung des jeweiligen Landes legen und gegebenenfalls in einem ersten Schritt eine Marktanalyse durchführen, um diese Bedürfnisse herauszufiltern. Was wollen die Leute dort? Was brauchen die Leute? Was würden die Leute kaufen? Chinesen kaufen andere Sachen als Europäer.*

IV. Social Media Marketing in BRIC countries

Trost: Do you think it's inevitable to enter social media networks as a marketing strategy when entering foreign country markets?

Offer: *Ja, auf jeden Fall! Das ist eine gute Methode, um sich schnell ein positives Image zu erarbeiten. Allerdings kann das mit der falschen Strategie auch nach hinten losgehen: Da im Social Media sehr viel miteinander vernetzt ist, geht es nicht nur auf einem Kanal hoch her, sondern es wird auch auf anderen Kanälen wie z.B. Twitter, Blogs, YouTube, etc. über das Unternehmen diskutiert, egal ob positiv oder negativ.*

Trost: For which companies do you think it's the most important to be active in social networks?

Offer: *Ich denke, alle Unternehmen haben da gleiche Chancen. Grundsätzlich ist es für jedes Unternehmen sinnvoll, um sich präsentieren und darstellen zu können.*

Trost: Imagine the following scenario: You are the social media marketing officer of a global German brand who wants to improve its social media activity in the networks of the BRIC countries (Brazil, Russia, India, China). Which steps would you take?

Offer: *Also erst einmal lege ich mir eine entsprechende Strategie zurecht, nachdem ich mich über das Land und die Gesellschaft informiert habe. Dann entscheide ich, welchen Content ich bereitstellen möchte. Je nachdem, was ich durch vorherige Forschung herausgefunden habe, erarbeite ich Themen, die die Leute interessieren, um sie dann entsprechend* *über meine Seite anzusprechen und für mein Unternehmen und meine Produkte zu gewinnen. Dann würde ich mit meiner Seite starten und diese bewerben, um ihren Bekanntheitsgrad zu erhöhen.*

Trost: What is the main criterion to consider?

Offer: *Als Unternehmen muss ich guten Content liefern und verstärkt in den Dialog mit den Fans treten. Das ist grundsätzlich das Wichtigste in sozialen Netzwerken.*

Trost: What do you think about the future development of social media marketing in the BRIC countries?

Offer: *Ich denke, das wird für Firmen, die in diesen Ländern erfolgreich agieren wollen, auf jeden Fall ein wichtiger Erfolgsfaktor sein.*

V. Prospect and Review

Trost: Do you have any questions from your side or further remarks?

Offer: *No, not really, nicht wirklich.*

XI. Interview III

Interview III
Date: 16.03.2012, 13.30h – 14.15h
Participant: **Alex Buchanan**

I. General information about the interviewee

Trost: How old are you?

Buchanan: *Ich bin 33 Jahre alt.*

Trost: How long have you been active in the field of social media and what is your experience?

Buchanan: *Ich war früher Marketingleiter bei Kwick.de, direkt nach dem Studium. Ich kenne Social Networks auch aus der Seite eines Betreibers, das heißt ich kenne die Mechanismen, wie User untereinander agieren und wie Mechanismen insgesamt in sozialen Netzwerken sind, dass Dinge geteilt werden, dass sich Leute vernetzen, etc. In der Zwischenzeit haben wir uns selbstständig gemacht und beraten jetzt große Unternehmen dabei, wie sie mit Social Media Erfolg haben. Wir beraten mit dem Schwerpunkt: Wie kann man gezielt Umsatz damit generieren, wie gewinnt man Mitarbeiter, wie bindet man Kunden durch Aktivitäten in sozialen Netzwerken.*

Trost: What is your current position?

Buchanan: *Jetzt bin ich Geschäftsführer und Unternehmensberater in meiner eignen Firma.*

II. Development of Social Media

Trost: Why do you think people are using social media?

Buchanan: *Social Media ist meiner Meinung nach nur das virtuelle Abbild des ganz normalen Lebens. Leute versuchen, sich selber darzustellen, versuchen Kontakte zu halten mit Leuten. Das ist wie im normalen Leben. Die Leute versuchen sich zu positionieren und das machen sie mit ganz unterschiedlichen Prioritäten, das kann aus Flirtgesichtspunkten, um eine spezielle soziale Stellung zu bekommen oder einen speziellen Expertenstatus in einem bestimmten beruflichen Gebiet geschehen. Alles entwickelt sich in den sozialen Netzwerken so wie auch im ganz normalen Leben. Die Leute geben Statusmeldungen von sich, einer positioniert sich als Quatschbacke, der andere postet nur Dinge die wirklich relevant und interessant sind. Früher hat man, um Leute neidisch zu machen, eine schöne Postkarte geschickt oder schöne Bilder gezeigt, heutzutage macht man ein Bild von dem tollen Pool, stellt es online und fragt: "Was macht ihr so?" Und das machen die Leute immer aus einem* *bestimmten Motiv. Zuerst macht man mit, weil jeder teilnimmt, aber schnell kristallisiert sich raus, was sein eigenes Ziel ist in den sozialen Netzwerken. Das wird auch weiterhin zunehmen, aber letzten Endes ist es einfach nur ein Abbild des realen Lebens. Manche Leute haben im realen Leben ein dickes Auto und positionieren sich dadurch. Und diese virtuellen Statussymbole werden umso mehr zunehmen je mehr die Leute in Social Networks sind. Man muss sich persönlich irgendwie darstellen. Man muss besser sein als die anderen und das macht man entweder durch Postings, Bilder etc. oder, indem man seine Karriere angibt, etc. So, wie das im normalen Leben auch ist.*

Trost: What do you think about the development of social media in general? Do you think social media will grow further with the same speed? Where do you see the endpoint of social media?

Buchanan: *Ich denke, dass die Art der Nutzung mehr in unseren Alltag integriert wird. Als Beispiel "spotify", diese open Graph Apps auf Facebook. Spotify, das ist ein Musikdienst, wo ich mich anmelden kann und umsonst online Musik hören kann. Das Ganze ist solange für mich kostenlos, solange ich erlaube, dass auf meiner Facebook Seite gepostet wird was ich gerade höre. Und ich denke in genau diese Richtung geht es weiter, dass man immer mehr veröffentlicht, was man gerade tut, um sich darüber zu unterhalten. Es wird immer mehr in den Alltag integriert. Auch durch das semantische Web wird es möglich, Dinge miteinander in Relation zu setzen. Das Web wird sozusagen intelligenter.*
Einen Endpunkt sehe ich nicht. Ich bin der Meinung, dass was dort passiert ist eigentlich nur ein Abbild dessen, was in der realen Welt passiert. Es wird alles weiter zusammenwachsen und ich denke nicht, dass es irgendeinen Endpunkt gibt. Ich sehe es nicht als eine Art Kanal, der irgendwann aufhört, sondern einfach nur als ein Abbild, wie schon gesagt, des ganz normalen Lebens.
Also, wenn jetzt beispielsweise ein Unternehmen wissen möchte, ob es Social Media überhaupt braucht, sagen wir immer, dass es ist kein Werbekanal ist. Sondern die Frage, die sich die Unternehmen da stellen, ist eigentlich die gleiche Frage als bräuchte ich ein Telefon: Es ist einfach ein weiterer Informationskanal. Es gibt beispielsweise amerikanische Unternehmen, die schon gar keine Emailadressen mehr vergeben, denn die Nutzung von Nachrichtenfunktionen in sozialen Netzwerken haben Emails schon längt wieder überholt.

Trost: For which aspects do you think social media could be used and in which direction do you think social media is going to develop (socializing, business, etc.)?

Buchanan: *Bezüglich Business: Genau da bin ich weiterhin der Meinung, dass es egal ist, in welchem Segment die Unternehmen tätig sind. Es ist nützlich für alle Unternehmen. Die Freundeskreise in sozialen Netzwerken sind auch weitestgehend homogenisiert, das hieβt, ich habe über Social Media die Möglichkeit, mir ein eigenes kleines Netzwerk aufzubauen, wo ich mit meiner Zielgruppe relativ eng kommunizieren kann, anstatt die Leute einzeln per Post zu kontaktieren.*

Trost: Where do you see chances, challenges and limits of social media for global German companies, e.g. BMW, adidas, NIVEA?

Buchanan: *Die Chancen sind natürlich eine viel größere Masse an Menschen zu erreichen und das zu einem viel geringeren Preis. Als Beispiel die Blendtec, die über die Community Facebook etc. abstimmt, was sie als nächstes durch den Mixer jagen sollen. Die User haben abgestimmt, das mit einem iPhone zu machen, und ca. 40 Mio. Leute haben dieses Video gesehen. Und in diesem Jahr, als das Video veröffentlicht wurde, haben sie ihrem Umsatz um 700 % gesteigert. Also, um diese Anzahl von Menschen zu erreichen, hätte man früher sehr sehr viel Geld bezahlt. Jetzt kann man es für relativ wenig Geld realisieren, weil die Leute untereinander vernetzt sind und Dinge, die gut sind, miteinander teilen.*
Risiken gibt es natürlich auch. Wenn die Firmen von der Unternehmenskultur her nicht offen sind, haben sie natürlich Schwierigkeiten. Man bekommt von seiner Zielgruppe eine unmittelbare Rückmeldung. Das Marketing, das man macht, muss mehr auf Augenhöhe geführt werden, man muss die Sprache seiner Zielgruppe sprechen und kennen. Was noch ein Risiken darstellt, ist, dass die Welt kleiner wird und damit auch die Konkurrenz eindeutiger für die Firmen direkt.

Trost: Granovetter, an American sociologist, stresses in his study "the strength of weak ties", that within social networks, the flow of information is increased through the existence of weak ties. What are the main success factors for a global company to use these weak ties successfully?

Buchanan: *Wenn man diesen Netzwerkfaktor in einer guten Form hinbekommen möchte, muss man den Leuten etwas bieten, etwas was die Leute erstens interessiert und zweitens was die Leute zu teilen bereit sind. Ich muss einen Mechanismus entwickeln, der die Leute dazu bringt, den Inhalt zu teilen. Dann werde ich großen Erfolg haben und diese weak ties gut nutzen können. Social Media wird von vielen Unternehmen noch als Werbekanal genutzt und das ist falsch. Man braucht eine klare Strategie dahinter und möchte, dass die Leute den Content teilen. Ich brauche also auch vernünftigen Inhalt dahinter und kann nicht nur einmal die Woche posten, wie toll das Wetter mal wieder ist.*

III. Social Media Marketing

Trost: What are the main aspects of social media which differ this marketing channel from others such as TV, radio, newspapers, etc.?

Buchanan: *Ein großer Unterschied hier ist natürlich das Geld. Es kostet einiges weniger. Ich habe die Möglichkeit eine Werbung mit integrierter Marktwerbung auf die Beine zu stellen, ich kann was posten und ich bekomme eine unmittelbare Rückmeldung darauf, ich kann dafür sorgen, dass Leute mit mir interagieren. Pepsi hat das zum Beispiel in den USA gemacht und haben ihre Community gefragt, wo sie für einen guten Zweck spenden könnten.*
Über Social Media hat man die Möglichkeit, den Markt mitbestimmen zu lassen was er will. Man kann also so auch das Scheitern von Produkten minimieren. Man muss also mit seinen

Leuten in der Sprache der Zielgruppe auf Augenhöhe kommunizieren, um erfolgreicher zu werden.

Trost: Which criteria are crucial when measuring success for companies, entering social networks as a marketing strategy (likes, comments etc.)?

Buchanan: *Was man auf jeden Fall nicht machen sollte, ist, dass man es an der Anzahl von Fans mißt, da es immer wieder Aktionen der Unternehmen gibt, die Aktionen starten wie: "jeder der uns heute liked, bekommt etwas umsonst." Von daher ist das nicht wirklich aussagekräftig und nicht sehr repräsentativ.*

Trost: When entering social networks as a global company, which main aspecmts have to be considered?

Buchanan: *Jedes Unternehmen muss natürlich seinen eigenen Weg finden. Aber was generell am Ende immer zählt sind die Verkaufszahlen, der Umsatz des Unternehmens.*

Trost: Do you think the social media activity of a global brand should be adapted to different countries (e.g. having different fan pages for different countries, in order to adapt to culture, or one page)?

Buchanan: *Think global, act local! Die Leute ticken natürlich komplett anders. Wenn ich zum Beispiel nach China gehe, stehe ich mit meiner Firma vor ganz anderen Herausforderungen. Man muss natürlich immer auf das Land eingehen und einstellen. In Frankreich herrscht beispielsweise eine relativ große BlogKultur, etc.*

Trost: What are the key success factors for local adaption in social media (national models, traditions, use of local language, etc.)?

Buchanan: *Es kommt natürlich immer auf die Branche an. Das ist eine Sache der Marktforschung, wie die Leute dort reagieren. Wieder ein Abbild der Realität. Also wie man im realen Leben handelt, so sollte man natürlich dann auch im sozialen Netzwerk handeln.*

IV. Social Media Marketing in BRIC countries

Trost: Do you think it's inevitable to enter social media networks as a marketing strategy when entering foreign country markets?

Buchanan: *Ja, definitiv. Besser bekommen Sie natürlich keine Rückmeldung als durch soziale Netzwerke. Die unverblümte tatsächliche Wahrheit und Reaktion auf Ihr Produkt bekommen Sie nur durch eine unmittelbare Reaktion von ihrer Zielgruppe.*

Trost: For which companies do you think it's the most important to be active in social networks?

Buchanan: *Bezüglich bestimmter Branchen in Social Networks würde ich sagen: nein. Wie gesagt, ein Abbild der Realität- jedes Unternehmen sollte in irgendeiner Form in den sozialen Netzwerken aktiv sein, aber natürlich sollte hier eine Strategie dahinter stehen, wie ich tatsächlich meine Ziele durch Social Media erreiche-. Aber ich würde nicht sagen, dass es Branchen gibt, die sich nicht dafür eignen. Es gibt Branchen für die eignen sich vielleicht bestimmt Netzwerke besser als andere, aber generell ist die Präsenz ein Muss.*

Trost: Imagine the following scenario: You are the social media marketing officer of a global German brand who wants to improve its social media activity in the networks of the BRIC countries (Brazil, Russia, India, China). Which steps would you take? And what is the main criterion to consider?

Buchanan: *Zuerst würde ich immer schauen, was es schon gibt. Es gibt zum Beispiel einen Menschen, der eine BMW-Seite hat, die schon so und so viele tausend Menschen als Fans hat. Wo hat also eine Privatperson, die hinter meinem Unternehmen steht, schon was gemacht. Wenn jemand eine Fanseite meines Unternehmens mit sehr vielen Fans hat, dann ist es auch dringend notwendig, diesem Menschen die nötige Beachtung zu schenken. Und es passiert oft, dass Leute Fan-Seiten gründen, die hinter einer Firma stehen und sich in ihrer Firma darum kümmern. Diese Menschen vermarkten quasi das Produkt. Viele Firmen haben diesen Punkt einfach schon verpasst und heute bezahlen sie dann viel Geld, um sich Rat zu holen, wie die ihre Firma einfach ein bisschen präsenter in den sozialen Netzwerken machen können. Und um solche Leute muss ich mich einfach jetzt kümmern. Damit würde ich persönlich auf jeden Fall anfangen.*
Es ist auch oft so, dass die Unternehmen sich nicht wirklich trauen, in soziale Netzwerke einzutreten, weil sie Angst vor negativen Rückmeldungen oder Kritik haben. Ich sollte also gucken, dass diese Kritik dort stattfindet, wo ich auch einen gelenkten Einfluss darauf habe und reagieren kann. Man sollte aber natürlich immer ein klares Ziel dahinter haben, wenn man in soziale Netzwerke eintritt.

Trost: What do you think about the future development of social media marketing in the BRIC countries?

Buchanan: *Ich denke das Endziel ist, dass jeder in diesen sozialen Netzwerken sein wird. Die Leute kommunizieren darüber, die Leute kommunizieren über Produkte. Ich denke, die Entwicklung ist die Gleiche wie in anderen Ländern auch. Aber die BRIC Länder haben wahrscheinlich noch mehr Priorität in die sozialen Netzwerke einzutreten, da es einfach immer mehr Arbeitsplätze gibt, die nicht mehr an Zeit und Ort gebunden sind.*

V. Prospect and Review

Trost: Do you have any questions from your side or further remarks?

Buchanan: *Nein, das war es eigentlich. Ich glaube jetzt habe ich schon lange geredet.*

Trost: Super Herr Buchanan, dann bedanke ich mich bei Ihnen und wünsche ihnen ein schönes Wochenende.

XII. Interview IV

Interview IV
Date: 28.03.2012, 11:00h – 11:45h
Participant: **Marc-Sven Kopka**

I. General information about the interviewee

Trost: May I ask you for your age?

Kopka: *Mein Alter ist 43 Jahre.*

Trost: How long have you been active in the field of social media and what is your experience?

Kopka: *Nun, in strengere Hinsicht seitdem ich bei XING arbeite, seit zweieinhalb Jahren also ungefähr. In privater Hinsicht deutlich länger. Meinen ersten Account in einem Social Network hatte ich bei XING ca. 2004, also ich bin schon seit einiger Zeit persönlich aktiv, ja.*

Trost: What is your current position?

Kopka: *Ich bin Vice President für* Corporate Communications bei XING.

II. Development of Social Media

Trost: Why do you think people are using social media?

Kopka: *Nach Aristoteles ist der Mensch ein soziales Wesen. Wenn man sich die Entwicklung der Art und Weise, wie Menschen mit ihrem Netzwerk, mit ihrer Umgebung, mit anderen Menschen Kontakt halten anguckt, stellt man fest, dass es ein paar tausend Jahre lang Kontakte gab mit Menschen, mit denen man spricht und die man treffen konnte.*
Ungefähr 1520 wurde der Brief erfunden und man konnte Kontakt halten, sich austauschen mit Menschen, die weit entfernt wohnten und das war sehr erfolgreich. Die Post ist zum Beispiel daraus hervorgegangen, und das sind große und vor allem erfolgreiche Unternehmen. Der Mensch hat also offenbar ein Bedürfnis, mit anderen Leuten in Kontakt zu bleiben. Dann passierte wiederum ganz lange Zeit nichts bis ca. in den 70er 80er Jahren, als die Email entstanden ist. Und dann seit ein paar Jahren Social Media. Es ist noch nicht so viel passiert, wenn man sich das überlegt. Soziale Medien sind deshalb erfolgreich, weil es ein Grundbedürfnis ist, sich mit anderen Menschen auszutauschen. Hier begegnet man einem Grundbedürfnis des Menschen.

Trost: And what do you think about the development of social media in general? Do you think social media will grow further with the same speed? Where do you see the endpoint of social media?

Kopka: *Social Media sind digitale Medien, digitale Plattformen zum Kommunikations- und Informationsaustausch zwischen Menschen.*
Ich glaube, auch wenn man sich die Geschichte anschaut, dass wir uns noch sehr stark am Anfang befinden. Wenn Sie sich beispielsweise XING als Social Network angucken, das es noch nicht so lange gibt, und was sich hier in den letzten 8 Jahren getan hat, ist Wahnsinn, unglaublich. Und die Entwicklung ist nicht absehbar. Ich denke, dass sich ganz viele Bedürfnisse und ganz viele interessante Anwendungen entwickeln werden.
Hier spielt meiner Meinung nach Lokalität eine ganz wichtige Rolle, denn letzten Endes lebt der Mensch in seiner eigenen lokalen Community, wo Sprache eine große Rolle spielt. Natürlich gibt es immer eine Ausnahme, aber für die meisten Nutzer spielt dieser Ansatz eine wichtige Rolle.
Aber wir stehen noch ganz am Anfang der Entwicklung und das wird auch in der Geschwindigkeit noch eine ganze Zeit so weitergehen. Ich denke, es kann niemand absehen, ob und wann es eine Art Endpunkt gibt.

Trost: For which aspects do you think social media could be used and in which direction do you think social media is going to develop (socializing, business, etc.)?

Kopka: *Was ein klarer Trend ist, ist der hin zur Mobilität, Stichwort Smartphone. In unserer Firma haben wir zum Beispiel fast ein Viertel unseres "Traffics" auf Smartphones und die Entwicklung hin zur Mobilität ist ganz rasant. Wenn Sie davon ausgehen, dass in ungefähr einem Jahr mehr Smartphones und mobile Geräte verkauft werden als Desktoprechner und Laptops, ist das eine sehr interessante Entwicklung. Und auch die Weiterentwicklung dieser mobilen Geräte, die vielleicht irgendwann gar keine Telefone mehr sind, wird auch dazu führen, dass die Tatsache, dass man miteinander vernetzt ist, nicht nur dann der Fall ist, wenn man gerade sein Mobile anschaltet oder am Rechner sitzt, sondern permanent. Es gibt ja schon sehr interessante Ideen, in andere Geräten, Brillen, etc. neue Technologien einzubauen. Und diese permanente Vernetzung wird natürlich Auswirkungen haben, die noch nicht abzusehen sind.*

Trost: Abgesehen von der Mobilität, inwiefern sehen sie die Entwicklung bezüglich Business?

Kopka: *Natürlich spielt es dort auch eine große Rolle, außer Frage. Unternehmen müssen da sein, wo ihre Kunden sind. Und schauen sie sich mal an, was das meist genutzte Medium ist: das Internet. Und was macht man am meisten im Internet: Social Media. Social Media hat alle anderen Anwendungen überholt, das heißt, die haben keine andere Chance als da zu sein, wo ihre Kunden sind.*

Trost: Where do you see chances, challenges and limits of social media for global German companies, e.g. BMW, adidas, NIVEA?

Kopka: *Die Herausforderung ist, dass das, was was man früher Öffentlichkeitsarbeit nannte, heute etwas völlig anderes ist. Der Begriff der Öffentlichkeitsarbeit hat sich sehr stark verändert. Früher wurde Öffentlichkeit dadurch definiert, dass öffentlicher Druck entstand, wenn fünf Leitmedien über dasselbe Thema geschrieben, beziehungsweise kritisiert haben. Sie konnten als guter Pressesprecher eines Unternehmens, indem Sie relative guten Kontakt zu vier bis fünf "Key-Journalisten" hatten, relativ gut Einfluss auf Berichterstattung und die öffentliche Wahrnehmung nehmen. Das war die Zeit der Massenmedien. Heute leben wir in der Zeit der Medienmassen. Jeder ist ein Stück weit selber Medium. Sie müssen viel stärker in den Dialog mit Kunden übergehen, nicht nur mit Medien, sondern mit Kunden und auch der interessierten Öffentlichkeit. Beispielsweise bei ING-DiBa, dass Dinge passieren können, die Sie überhaupt nicht absehen können, die aber eine direkte Wirkung auf ihre Wahrnehmung haben. Das heißt, dass das, was wir Öffentlichkeitsarbeit nennen, der Versuch ist, in den Dialog mit der Öffentlichkeit einzutreten, mit dem Versuch, ihre eigenen Interessen an bestimmte Wahrnehmungen binden zu lassen. Und dieser Vorgang ist deutlich komplizierter und wesentlich weniger steuerbar als in der Vergangenheit. Sie müssen im Prinzip keine Technik beherrschen, sondern Kulturtechnik, nämlich die Kulturtechnik der Kommunikation. Menschen dementsprechend zuhören, reagieren, und das nicht nach schematischen Vorgaben, sondern an die Situation angepasst. Das ist schon eine Herausforderung.*

Trost: Das heißt mich auch als Unternehmen anzupassen an die jeweiligen Länder, mit denen ich in Kontakt trete?

Kopka: *Absolut. Es ist ja ein Unterschied, ob ich jetzt ein Produkt in Hamburg oder in Saudi-Arabien verkaufe. Diese Anpassung liegt auf der Hand und sollte ganz klar verfolgt werden.*

Trost: Granovetter, an American sociologist, stresses in his study "the strength of weak ties", that within social networks, the flow of information is increased through the existence of weak ties. What are the main success factors for a global company to use these weak ties successfully?

Kopka: *Natürlich, Weak Ties sind vorhanden. Weak Ties ist ein Thema welches man sich auch sehr gut veranschaulichen kann. Die Information, die Ihr enges Netzwerk hat, ist wahrscheinlich relativ identisch. Sie suchen sich Ihre Kontakte nach ähnlichen Interessen, ähnlichen Erfahrungen, die mit denen Sie sowieso viel zu tun haben, aus. Da fließen Informationen, die allgemein bekannt sind, und da hat wahrscheinlich keiner eine Königsinformation.*

Nehmen wir aber nun einfach mal ein Beispiel: Ich hab keinerlei Beziehungen privater Natur zu Medizinfachleuten. Es kann natürlich sein, dass ich regelmäßig, einmal im Jahr, jemanden auf einer Veranstaltung treffe, der Lobbyist für ein medizinisches Unternehmen ist. Er ist nett, wir plaudern und das war's. In dem Moment, wo ich eine schwere Krankheit ha-

be und Rat über ein spezifisches medizinisches Thema brauche, mit Fachleuten sprechen möchte, dann ist sein Netzwerk für mich auf einmal total relevant. Das ist ein ganz praktisches und auch individuelles Beispiel, was direkt zeigt, dass die Weak Ties nicht nur eine Theorie sind. Man stellt festt, dass diese Weak Ties von unschätzbarer Bedeutung sind. Der Unterschied zur Vergangenheit ist, dass Social Networks diese Weak Ties nutzbar und transparent machen. Das war mir früher gar nicht bewusst, aber heute kann ich direkt sehen, mit wem Leute in Social Networks vernetzt sind, und kann diese Information nutzen. Und das ist ein großartiger Nutzen, der auch den Vorteil und Erfolg von sozialen Netzwerken mitunter erklärt.
Was heißt das für Firmen: Dieser Mechanismus der Weak Ties muss erstens verstanden werden und zweitens, die Vernetzung und die dadurch entstehende Komplexität, aber auch die Geschwindigkeit dessen, was die Öffentlichkeit unternimmt; letztendlich ihre Zielgruppe.

III. Social Media Marketing

Trost: What are the main aspects of social media which differ this marketing channel from others such as TV, radio, newspapers, etc.?

Kopka: *In Social Media haben Sie den Feedbackkanal. Wenn ich eine Anzeige schalte, dann schalte ich eine Anzeige und es passiert vorerst gar nichts.*
Wenn ich in Social Networks aktiv bin, habe ich direkte Feedbackkanäle, da antwortet mir jemand, dem wiederrum ich antworten muss. Das bekommen andere mit, die sich dann auch in diesen Dialog einschalten und unter Umständen entpuppt sich meine empfängerorientierte Botschaft als absenderorientiert und funktioniert vorne und hinten nicht. Das heißt, ich muss hier in Social Networks eine viel größere Offenheit haben, ich muss in der Lage sein auf Reaktionen zu reagieren und ich muss zum Dialog bereit sein und auch dialogfähig. Das ist ein ziemlich großer Aufwand und ein völlig anderer "Mindset". Das ist nicht: Ich kaufe mir eine Seite und definiere was darauf steht, sondern ich habe eine Social Network Seite und meine Stimme ist eine von vielen. Die Stimmt der Kunden und derjenigen, die sich an der Debatte beteiligen zählt genauso viel wie meine eigene. Und da das mehr sind als ich, ist meine Stimme, wie gesagt, nur einer von vielen. Ich habe keine größere Autorität mehr, nur eine größere Aufmerksamkeit. Letztendlich ist es hier ein völlig anderer Angang, ein völlig anderes Marketingkonzept.

Trost: Denken Sie, dass bezüglich der Marketingausgaben eines Unternehmens Social Media eine größere Bedeutung zukommen wird?

Kopka: *Pauschal ist das schwer zu beantworten. Wenn ich einen starken B2B Fokus habe und weltweit von sechshundert Kunden lebe, nehmen wir an in Maschinenbau, etc., stellt sich die Frage, ob ich hier durch Marketing einen großen Mehrwert habe. Da geht es eher darum, dass ich Reputationspflege betreibe und gucke, wie meine Marke in sozialen Netzwerken und Medien wahrgenommen wird: meine Marke als Arbeitgeber, meine Marke als*

"corporate citizen", etc. Aber für die Kundenansprache funktioniert es in diesem Beispiel wahrscheinlich besser, wenn ich meine Kunden besuche.
Wenn wir Konsumgüter betrachten, sollte das Unternehmen natürlich vertreten sein, das Unternehmen ist tendenziell da, wo die Kunden sind und die Kunden sind hier in Social Media.

Trost: Also sollte jedes Unternehmen irgendwie in Social Media aktiv sein?

Kopka: *Ich würde sagen, dass jedes Unternehmen ohnehin in Social Media, Social Networks vertreten sind, auch ohne etwas zu tun, der Name wird sich finden. Das heißt, jedes Unternehmen befindet sich bereits in sozialen Netzwerken, die Frage ist: Will ich das, was über mich gesagt wird, beeinflussen oder nicht? Ich glaube jedes Unternehmen muss, und da bin ich wirklich bei jedem Unternehmen, mindestens "Monitoring" betrieben. Ich kann immer noch eingreifen, wenn ich ein Problem mit der Wahrnehmung habe, die da entsteht. Das jedoch in jeder Industrie eine gesteuerte, aktive und strategische Präsenz von Nöten ist, das würde ich nicht sagen, nein.*

Trost: Und bezüglich eines eigenständiges Departments für Social Media, was denken Sie?

Kopka: *Es kommt auf die Größe und Zielsetzung des Unternehmens an. Wenn Sie mehr "monitoren", kann es auch angedockt werden, aber es kommt immer darauf an. Es sollte natürlich immer eng miteinander abgestimmt sein. Sie brauchen auf jeden Fall eine dezidierte Verantwortlichkeit, ob das jetzt eine Person, mehrere, ob es eine eigene Unit ist oder irgendwo angedockt, das kann man pauschal so nicht beantworten.*

Trost: Ok, so which criteria are crucial when measuring success for companies, entering social networks as a marketing strategy (likes, comments, etc.)?

Kopka: *Ich bin kein Marketing-Fachmann, um da offen und ehrlich zu antworten. Hier würde ich aber sagen, es kommt drauf an. Die Frage ist, was mein Ziel ist. Wenn es mein Ziel ist mehr Produkte zu verkaufen, kann ich es nicht ganz sagen, wenn es mein Ziel ist eine bestimmte Wahrnehmung zu erzeugen, also letztendlich einen "Branding-Effect" zu erzielen, dann sind "Likes" und positive Comments aus meiner Sicht eine sinnvolle Messgröße. Und sonst müssen Sie letzten Endes eine "Marketingfunnel" definieren, wo Sie sagen, wie viel Aufmerksamkeit in den sozialen Medien führt eigentlich zu bestimmten Kaufverhalten. Und da wird wahrscheinlich nicht ein einfaches "Likes" und "Comments" zählen ausreichend, sondern hier brauchen Sie eine integrierte Marketingstrategie.*

Trost: When entering social networks as a global company, which main aspects have to be considered?

Kopka: *Definitiv, die lokalen Gegebenheiten muss ich hier beachten, die sprachlichen Gegebenheiten und dann brauche ich - ganz altmodisch - ein Ziel, ich brauche eine Vorstellung davon, wie weit ich vom Ziel entfernt bin, also wie ist die aktuelle Situation, wie ist das*

Ziel und dann ist die Frage, wie erreiche ich das Ziel und was ist meine Strategie. Und diese Strategie muss ich umsetzten und regelmäßig deren Erfolg messen. Ganz klassische, langweilige aber unersetzliche Vorgehensweise.

Trost: Genau das, was viele Unternehmen meiner Meinung nach noch nicht wirklich tun.

Kopka: *Ehrlich gesagt nein, das haben sie nicht, und wenn sie so etwas tun, das hört man schon raus, ist es Arbeit. Sie brauchen also jemand der das dezidiert tut, am besten ein Team, und sie brauchen ein Budget. Das ist glaube ich irreführend, wenn man glaubt, Social Media ist eine billige Variante, wo man nicht viel tun muss, es läuft von selbst und hat einen tollen Erfolg und eine großartige Präsenz. Das ist ein Trugschluss. Wenn man es professional machen will, muss man Zeit investieren.*

Trost: Do you think the social media activity of a global brand should be adapted to different countries (e.g. having different fan pages for different countries, in order to adapt to culture, or one page)?

Kopka: *Ich denke, es kommt auf das Produkt der Marke an, aber ja, es macht Sinn. Eine übergeordnete Präsenz zu haben, gleichzeitig auch regionale Präsenz die aufeinander abgestimmt, konsistent, aber nicht deckungsgleich sind. Ich denke schon, dass das Bedürfnis da ist und auch, dass unterschiedliche Märkte sehr zu berücksichtigen sind, auch wenn wir hier über globale Märkte sprechen. Es kann ein riesiger Unterschied sein ob ich mein Produkt in einem eher freizügigen oder konservativen Land vertreibe.*

Trost: What are the key success factors for local adaption in social media (national models, traditions, use of local language, etc.)?

Kopka: *Sprache natürlich, Kultur, total wichtig. Wir haben sogar schon einen Repräsentanten bei uns in der Firma in der deutschspracheigen Schweiz. Hier kann man schon sehen, dass es ein Unterschied ist, ob ein Deutscher in der Schweiz auftritt oder ein Schweizer. Es wird ganz anders akzeptiert. Er versteht die Kultur natürlich unmittelbar. Natürlich kann man sagen, dass Deutsche und Schweizer sich in der Kultur nicht so wahnsinnig unterscheiden, aber selbst wenn wir es hier schon feststellen, wie soll das dann für China, Brasilien, etc. gelten? Man kommt also nicht drum herum, ein Land wirklich zu verstehen. Das können am besten Leute, die aus diesem Land kommen.*

IV. Social Media Marketing in BRIC countries

Trost: Do you think it's inevitable to enter social media networks as a marketing strategy when entering foreign country markets?

Kopka: *Zuerst würde ich mir immer die Frage stellen wie entwickelt ist Social Media in diesem Land und wie ist das Mediennutzungsverhalten in diesem Land. Wenn ich davon* *ausgehe, dass es so ähnlich ist wie hier, dann würde ich sagen auf jeden Fall. Wenn es nicht so ist, muss man eine Strategie wählen, die dem jeweiligen Nutzungsverhalten entspricht.*

Trost: For which companies do you think it's the most important to be active in social networks?

Kopka: *Wie schon gesagt, "fast moving consumer goods", definitiv, da haben Sie glaube ich keine andere Chance, da müssen Sie aktiv sind. Wenn Sie im B2B Bereich aktiv sind, muss man sich das von vorne herein anders anschauen und hier kann man natürlich zu dem Schluss kommen, dass es nicht so wahnsinnig viel Sinn macht.*

Trost: Now, imagine the following scenario: You are the social media marketing officer of a global German brand who wants to improve its social media activity in the networks of the BRIC countries (Brazil, Russia, India, China). Which steps would you take?

Kopka: *Ich würde als erstes Kontakt aufnehmen mit Leuten, die diesen Markt kennen und würde versuchen zu verstehen, wie das Social Media Nutzungsverhalten ist, was das eigentlich für mich heißt und welche Strategie ich entwickeln muss. Also was ist mein Ziel, wie ist die Situation, was ist mein Ausgangspunkt und mit welchen Schritten kann ich diese Ziel erreichen? Dann einen entsprechenden Plan aufsetzten und das mit dem lokalen Know-how umsetzen.*

Trost: What is the main criterion to consider?

Kopka: *Kultur, als global-charakterlicher Begriff sicher, Kultur umfasst Sprache, Mediennutzungsverhalten, etc., ein ganz wesentlicher Punkt.*

Trost: What do you think about the future development of social media marketing in the BRIC countries?

Kopka: *Es tut mir leid, dazu kann ich keine kompetente Antwort geben, das vermag ich nicht zu beurteilen.*

V. Prospect and Review

Trost: Do you have any questions from your side or further remarks?

Kopka: *Nein, spannendes Thema, überhaupt keine Fragen. Wenn Sie fertig sind bin, ich neugierig, dann schicken Sie mir mal ein Link oder eine PDF.*

Trost: Ja super, danke.

XIII. Interview V

Interview V
Date: 30.03.2012, 09:00h – 09:45h
Participant: Dr. Alexandra Wöllenstein

I. General information about the interviewee

Trost: May I ask you for your age?

Wöllenstein: *Ich bin 36 Jahre alt.*

Trost: How long have you been active in the field of marketing and what is your experience?

Wöllenstein: *Nach dem Studium, also seit 12 Jahren jetzt. Zuerst habe ich für 5 Jahre als wissenschaftliche Mitarbeiterin an der Universität gearbeitet, am Lehrstuhl für Beschaffung und Produktpolitik im Bereich Marketing.*

Trost: What is your current position?

Wöllenstein: *Seit 7 Jahren bin ich in einer kleinen Unternehmensberatung, bei Stüwe in Langenfeld.*

II. Development of Social Media

Trost: Why do you think people are using social media?

Wöllenstein: *Privatpersonen nutzen Social Media natürlich, um Kontakte zu pflegen. Es kommt natürlich im starken Maße immer auf das Netzwerk an, ob es etwas wie XING ist, wo die Geschäftskontakte eher gepflegt werden, wobei das natürlich nicht nur darauf beschränkt ist, oder so etwas wie Facebook, was natürlich eher auf Privatkontakte ausgerichtet ist, um in Kontakte zu bleiben und informiert zu sein.*

Trost: And what do you think about the development of social media in general? Do you think social media will grow further with the same speed and where do you see the endpoint of social media, all from the perspective of marketing?

Wöllenstein: *Ohje, wenn man so etwas wüsste. Das hängt im starken Maße von der Technologie ab, wie die sich weiterentwickelt. Also, wenn ich mich daran zurückerinnere als ich in der Uni war, da war ein Notebook was ganz besonderes, und so alt bin ich nicht. Wenn man sich Filme anguckt, wie beispielsweise "zurück in die Zukunft", wo sie dann reisen in das Jahr 2013 oder 15, wie man sich damals die Zeit vorgestellt hat, dann ist es ja heute ganz anders. Ich glaube, dass das zurzeit schwer vorherzusagen ist, wie sich die Technik entwi-*

ckeln wird und was da für Durchbrüche kommen, was möglich wird. Ich denke, dass es nicht zum Stillstand kommen wird, warum sollte es. Die Leute sind ja immer daran interessiert weiter zu gehen aber wo das hingeht, ich glaube wer das in der Lage ist vorherzusehen hat ausgesorgt. Von daher ist das Ganze schwer abzuschätzen. Ich glaube, ich habe meinen ersten Account ca. 98 bekommen, und da war es noch ein Riesenakt mit Emails und Modems sich einzuwählen. Da hätte niemand gedacht, dass jetzt fast jeder so ein Smartphone hat, wo man sich mal eben so online einwählen kann. Von daher ist das ganz schwer für mich einzuschätzen.

Trost: For which aspects do you think social media could be used and in which direction do you think social media is going to develop (socializing, business, etc.)?

Wöllenstein: *Also, Social Media hört man ja überall. Das ist das Schlagwort. Ich bin in der Hinsicht ein wenig skeptisch, weil ich denke, dass es ganz toll, ganz modern ist und ganz viele Unternehmen einfach darauf anspringen, weil es einfach schick ist. Und für heute gesprochen glaube ich, dass viele Unternehmen irgendetwas machen, weil sie glauben es machen zu müssen, unabhängig davon, ob die Zielgruppe, die sie eigentlich ansprechen, dafür geeignet ist. Es gibt sicherlich Unternehmen, für die ist es mehr als notwendig, sich auch heute schon darin zu bewegen, einfach weil sie eine ganz junge Zielgruppe haben und weil es für die "digital natives", die jetzt auf die Welt kommen und damit quasi aufwachsen und für die Facebook der alltägliche Briefkasten wird, für die Unternehmen, die müssen auch heute schon dort vertreten sein. Andererseits gibt es ganz viele Unternehmen, die Social Media-Profile haben, wo überhaupt keine User dahinter stehen, einfach weil die Zielgruppe nicht affin für Social Media ist, und das bricht ganz klar irgendwo Mitte 30 schon ab.*
Also, wie viele Leute ich kenne, die überhaupt gar kein Facebook Profil haben, weil sie damit nicht aufgewachsen sind, weil sie demgegenüber skeptisch aufgrund desDatenschutz stehen, weil sie nicht wollen, dass alle immer wissen, was man gerade macht oder weil sie nicht alle Photos teilen wollen. Man muss das immer aus der Perspektive der Zielgruppe von heute sehen.
Ich glaube, dass es sich zukünftig Richtung Social Media entwickeln wird, weil natürlich die Jugend von heute die ältere Generation von morgen ist. Die erwarten das natürlich dann schon wieder. Es wird sich also ändern im Zeitverlauf.

Trost: Where do you see chances, challenges and limits of social media for global German companies, e.g. BMW, adidas, NIVEA?

Wöllenstein: *Es ist immer die Frage, wo sich meine Zielgruppe bewegt. Wenn sich meine Zielgruppe heute in Social Media befindet, kann ich sie auch darüber ansprechen. Wenn nicht, dann kann ich machen, was ich will und es wird nicht gesehen. Oder ich muss irgendwelche Mechanismen entwickeln, wie ich diese Leute dahin bekomme, wo ich sie haben will.*
Es wird immer nur darüber geredet, wie toll Social Media ist, aber was aus dem Blick verloren wird ist, dass es doch um die Zielgruppe geht und dass es doch darum geht, mit der Zielgruppe Umsatz zu machen. Und wenn man dann daran vorbeiläuft, bloß weil man

Social Media persönlich ganz toll findet, die Zielgruppe aber viel älter ist und nicht in Social Media vertreten, glaube ich, dass es wenig zielführend ist. Und das wird aus dem Blick verloren. Im Marketing muss man immer alles auf die Zielgruppe ausrichten.
Es nützt natürlich nichts, ein Profil in Social Media zu haben, wo gar keiner aktiv ist und da sollte man sich doch die Frage stellen, ob das nicht ein traurigeres Bild ist als hätte man einfach gar kein Profil. Es sollte also immer vor dem Hintergrund der jeweiligen Zielgruppe bewertet werden und das wird im Moment nicht immer getan. Social Media wird immer als der "Hype" dargestellt, weil es auch toll ist, weil es spannend ist, weil es ja auch alles junge Leute sind, die es nach vorne bringen, das ist gar keine Frage, ist alles toll, die Frage ist aber, passt es auf die Zielgruppe und das ist heute anders als es mal sein wird.

Trost: Granovetter, an American sociologist, stresses in his study "the strength of weak ties", that within social networks, the flow of information is increased through the existence of weak ties. What are the main success factors for a global company to use these weak ties successfully, especially considering the marketing aspect for companies?

Wöllenstein: *Was natürlich definitiv so ist, ist dass Informationen in sozialen Netzwerken extrem schnell verbreitet werden können. Das kann natürlich eine Riesenchance sein, das kann aber, und das muss den Unternehmen bewusst sein, auch zu absoluten Selbstläufer werden. Wenn jemand anfängt zu kritisieren oder Negatives zu posten, verbreitet sich das natürlich ganz genauso schnell. Das ist also Chance und Risiko zugleich. Hier muss sich ein Unternehmen dessen bewusst sein und natürlich auch im Notfall richtig reagieren. Und das glaube ich, haben die meisten nicht im Griff, wie man damit umgeht was einem nicht so gefällt.*

III. Social Media Marketing

Trost: What are the main aspects of social media which differ this marketing channel from others such as TV, radio, newspapers, etc.?

Wöllenstein: *Der eins zu eins Dialog, der im Social Media entstehen kann, ist natürlich ein Riesenunterschied. Ich kann TV sehen und mit dem Fernseher reden, aber es hört keiner, Radio hör ich mir an und das hört auch niemand, ich kann die Zeitung lesen und das hört auch niemand. Social Media hat den riesen Vorteil, dass ich als User sofort etwas zurückgeben kann. Ich kann also in den Dialog treten, "Face to Face". Das ist natürlich ein Riesenvorteil, aber auch eine Riesenaufgabe. Wenn ich als User dort etwas reingeben kann, dann habe ich auch die Erwartungshaltung, dass ich etwas zurückbekomme. Nur wenn das auch richtig umgesetzt wird, ist das eine Chance für das Unternehmen, ansonsten ist das auch ein Risiko.*

Trost: Denken Sie, dass bezüglich der Marketingausgaben eines Unternehmens Social Media eine größere Bedeutung zukommen wird?

Wöllenstein: *Es hängt natürlich von der Konservativität des Unternehmens ab. Prinzipiell würde ich sagen, dass alle das haben wollen und alle mitmachen wollen, ohne groß darüber nachzudenken.*
Und ich denke, wenn jemand mit einem tollen Social Media Projekt kommt, egal ob es zielführend für das Unternehmen ist oder nicht, wird es wahrscheinlich immer recht leicht sein, es im Unternehmen zu positionieren, weil die Leute es einfach schick finden. Ich bin der Überzeugung, dass hier viel Geld ausgegeben wird, obwohl es nicht immer richtig angelegt ist, sagen wir so.

Trost: Von welchen Unternehmen sollte Social Media genutzt werden?

Wöllenstein: *Alle Unternehmen, die sich an die ganz junge Zielgruppe richten, weil die sie dort erreichen. Die können ja alleine von dem, was sie an Feedback kriegen so viel lernen, dass die da auf jeden Fall vertreten sein sollten. Einfach weil das einer von den Orten ist, wo die Zielgruppe sich immer aufhält und man sie immer erreichen kann und wo man ja unglaublich viel drüber lernen kann, sagen wir so bis Anfang 30. Für die, die andere Zielgruppen haben, ist es mittel- bis langfristig im Kopf zu behalten, aber nicht kurzfristig umzusetzen.*

Trost: Ok, so which criteria are crucial when measuring success for companies, entering social networks as a marketing strategy (likes, comments, etc.)?

Wöllenstein: *Es ist die Frage, welches Ziel ich habe. Wenn es darum geht, dass die Leute einfach über meine Marke reden, dann reicht es ja schon, wenn ich sehe, wie viele Leute reagieren, wenn ich es aber natürlich an Umsatz messen will, dann ist es etwas schwieriger. Nur weil viel von mir geredet wird muss ja nicht direkt viel von mir gekauft werden.*

Trost: When entering social networks as a global company, which main aspects have to be considered?

Wöllenstein: *Die Zielgruppe. Sich bewusst zu sein wie man damit umgeht, wenn etwas nicht so läuft wie es soll. Wenn ich viele Beschwerden bekomme, muss ich auch wissen, wie ich damit umzugehen habe. Es sollte nicht so sein, dass auf einmal irgendwelche User dafür bezahlt werden, dass sie etwas für mich posten, was ja auch schon vorgekommen ist. Da verliert man seine Authentizität. Man sollte als Unternehmen eine Strategie haben und wissen, wie man damit umgeht.*

Trost: Denken sie, es ist wichtig ein eigenständiges Department für Social Media zu haben, oder eher nicht?

Wöllenstein: *Es hängt natürlich immer von der Größe des Unternehmens ab. Es sollte natürlich immer gucken, wie integriere ich so etwas in das Marketing, denn hier sollte es Hand in Hand übergehen. Social Media ist ja im Grunde nichts anderes als ein Vermarktungsinstrument.*

Trost: Do you think the social media activity of a global brand should be adapted to different countries (e.g. having different fan pages for different countries, in order to adapt to culture, or one page)?

Wöllenstein: *Viele Unternehmen haben natürlich auch für viele Slogans, Werbungen, Variationen des Markennamens in anderen Ländern. Wenn man so differenziert in der Markenbearbeitung ist, liegt es natürlich auch nahe, differenzierte Profile zu machen, weil ich das ja alleine schon wegen des Markennamens tun muss. Sobald ich es global mache, muss ich mich natürlich auch immer fragen, ob es in den kulturellen Kontext passt.*

Trost: What are the key success factors for local adaption in social media (national models, traditions, use of local language, etc.)?

Wöllenstein: *Ich frage mich, ob es plausible ist, wenn jemand der in Amerika sitzt und eine Fanpage in Indien oder Brasilien betreut, auch wirklich darauf eingehen kann. Eigentlich heißt es doch, dass der direkte Kontakt zum Konsumenten aufgebaut werden soll. Es sollte also immer alles vor Ort angepasst werden, um auch auf die Begebenheiten eingehen zu können.*
Es sollte immer jemand lokal vor Ort sein. Alleine schon wegen der Zeitverschiebung um direkt antworten zu können, wie redet man, wie geht man mit den Leuten um.

IV. Social Media Marketing in BRIC countries

Trost: Do you think it's inevitable to enter social media networks as a marketing strategy when entering foreign country markets?

Wöllenstein: *Das hängt natürlich wieder von der Zielgruppe ab. Ich würde mir angucken wie die Leute, die ich ansprechen will, dort in Social Media aktiv sind. Wenn ja, dann ist das ein Instrument, was ich gut benutzen kann. Meiner Meinung nach muss ich gucken, ob sich die Zielgruppe dort bewegt.*

Trost: Denken Sie es gibt einen Unterscheid für B2B und B2C Unternehmen, aktiv Social Media Marketing zu betreiben?

Wöllenstein: *Es gibt bestimmt bestimme Einzelfalle bei B2B, wo man sagt, das macht auch Sinn, beispielsweise zur Mitarbeiterrekrutierung. Aber generell würde ich sagen, dass die B2C Unternehmen eher betroffen davon sind als die im B2B Bereich. Es hängt aber natürlich auch von der Plattform ab.*

Trost: Now, imagine the following scenario: You are the social media marketing officer of a global German brand who wants to improve its social media activity in the networks of the BRIC countries (Brazil, Russia, India, China). Which steps would you take?

Wöllenstein: *Ich würde mir die kulturellen Hintergründe als Erstes angucken. Auch um zu sehen, ob ich meine Strategie an die Zielgruppe anpassen muss und wenn ja, wie ich hier vorgehen sollte.*

Trost: What is the main criterion to consider?

Wöllenstein: *Ich muss meine Zielgruppe erreichen. In Social Media sollte ich deswegen aktiv sein, um es als systematisches Marketinginstrument zu nutzen und um die Umsatzziele zu erreichen. Und dann muss Social Media ja auch auf meine Zielgruppe ausgerichtet sein.*

Trost: What do you think about the future development of social media marketing in the BRIC countries?

Wöllenstein: *Da wird sicherlich eine Menge passieren, genauso wie hier in Deutschland, weil Social Media natürlich auch immer mehr in den Alltag übergehen wird. Langfristig müssen sich alle Unternehmen Gedanken darüber machen, wie sie damit umgehen werden und auf jeden Fall eine Strategie entwickeln, was sie dort tun oder auch nicht tun möchten. Es kann ja auch eine ganz fundierte Entscheidung dagegen sein. Und das gleiche gilt für die BRIC Länder. Man muss sich immer angucken, wie will ich hier agieren und was erfordert die Kultur und die Zielgruppe von mir.*

V. Prospect and Review

Trost: Do you have any questions from your side or further remarks?

Wöllenstein: *Nein, aber spannendes Thema. Ich hoffe, dass ich ein bisschen helfen konnte.*

Trost: Ja, auf jeden Fall, danke.

XIV. Interview VI

Interview VI

Date: 19.04.2012, 17:00h – 17:45h
Participant: Jorge Junior

I. General information about the interviewee

Trost: May I ask you for your age?

Junior: *Yeah, I am 28.*

Trost: How long have you been active in the field of marketing and what is your experience?

Trost: What is your experience with social media and your current position?

Junior: *In my recent jobs, I was in charge of their social media activities like blogs, etc., and currently I am working as a marketing analyst at BMW in Brazil. I am also responsible for the social media marketing for BMW as well as MINI.*

II. Development of Social Media

Trost: Why do you think people are using social media?

Junior: *People are using social media, because it's fun. They want to get in contact and like to stay connected. They are also doing research. In Brazil, people are spending a lot of time in social networks, playing games, commenting, sharing photos etc. They are just doing everything in social media.*

In the past, the most important social media network was Orkut, but now it's Facebook. Facebook is ahead of Orkut. Facebook has much more people and more and more are getting connected on Facebook also with their mobile phones, so always being there.

Trost: And what do you think about the development of social media in general? Do you think social media will grow further with the same speed?

Junior: *It's the future.*

Trost: Where do you see the biggest chance for BMW being active in social media networks?

Junior: *Monitoring is one of the most important aspects. Here we can directly learn from the people and our customers. We are really active. We can stay directly engaged with our customers, because they are telling us, if they are happy or not. So it's a great platform to share information. We are showing them by our history and technology what we are doing and the fans are really active in our social network.*

Trost: *How do you react concerning negative posts on your social media site Facebook-BMW Brazil?*

Junior: *Well, most of the time, if people are posting something which is negative like "I prefer Audi instead of BMW", the fans of the social network are directly reacting on their own. So it's interesting to see how all the BMW fans are reacting and solving the issue on their own.*

III. Social Media Marketing at BMW Brazil

Trost: What is the main aspect why you are using social media marketing?

Junior: *As BMW is a premium brand, we want to inform people with information about our product, so mainly it's about branding. We have a DNA and we want to tell people about our brand.*

Trost: Within your company, do you see the presence in social media networks as a marketing channel like TV, radio or newspaper to inform people or as even more?

Junior: *We can directly learn from people here. But it always depends. Every feature has its time. We had the journal, the radio, the TV and now it's the time of the Internet and social media. So you have to be active and present here. In the end everything will be combined, and that's what's happening at the moment. We have to be everywhere, because some people are more conservative and prefer being informed via newspaper.*
But concerning social media, it's like a movie. It just came up some years ago so nobody know how to behave in the right way. Everything is changing all the time.

Trost: How are you measuring your success of social media network?

Junior: *At Facebook it's great, because when creating a company page, you can directly see how many people are engaging, talking about you, the growth, the range, etc. I think this is the future. There are several statistics which can be used to be informed directly about your social media activity. You have all these information in the background and can use them directly.*

Trost: Do you have a separate department for social media activities at your company BMW Brazil?

Junior: *At the moment social media is included in marketing here. But the interaction between the departments is of high importance. Because everything we post on Facebook comes from different departments which knows the best. So if we talk about some technical information, we also speak before with the engineers. And if someone has questions about jobs, they will communicate via social media to the Human Resources. So through our page, you stay in contact with the other departments.*

IV. Specific Questions to BMW Brazil

Trost: I found out that BMW has not only a global brand, but also local pages such as BMW Brazil. Why did you choose this approach?

Junior: *We are adapting. In Brazil, not everyone is speaking English, so if we have just the international page, people are not able to interact. Here they can directly post and we can answer questions in Portuguese, which is really important. Information in Portuguese are directed to our target group here in Brazil.*
We have a global content when telling people all about the brand, but it's always locally adapted.

Trost: Ok, and BMW is a German brand. Along a survey, it was found out that the German image is appreciated in the BRIC countries, including Brazil. Do you use German images?

Junior: *Well, we are using the models, yes. And I think everybody knows that it's a German brand, so here we are more adapting to the culture as in terms of language. We don't push that BMW is German. I would say that we have much more than just being German.*

Trost: Concerning job recruitment. Do you already use your Facebook page in order to announce job vacancies?

Junior: *At the moment we are trying to think about a strategy. We are seeing Facebook more as a socializing tool and concerning job offers, "linked in" is used more here.*

V. Prospect and Review

Trost: Do you have any questions from your side or further remarks?

Junior: *It's a great topic. You are doing research not only for the present, but also for the future. This is amazing. So I would be more than happy, if you could send me your study with the results of BMW Brazil. And if you have any questions, you can call me anytime.*

Trost: Ok that's great. Yeah, I will send you my study as soon as it is ready. So thank you very much for your insights.

XV. Results of the Quantitative Analysis – BMW

BMW	**08.03.2012**				
Country	***Network***	***Page***	***Group***	#	***Description***
BRAZIL					
	Facebook	**15 results found**			
		BMW BRASIL Cars		124.775	likes
		BMW Motorrad Brasil Product/Service		2.906	likes
		BMW Riders - Brasil		113	likes
		BMW F800 R - Brasil		52	likes
		BMW Riders - Brasil		22	likes
		BMW do Brasil Company		19	likes
		BMW Brasil Community		13	likes
		BMW 1150 Adventure Brasil Enternatinment		12	likes
		S1000RR-BMW-BRASIL		8	likes
		BMW do Brasil Local Business		8	likes
			7 results found		
			BMW Car Club Brasil Closed group	2.654	members
			BMW MOTO BRASIL Closed group	143	members
			GRUPO BRASIL BMW G650GS Open group	70	members
			BMW Clube Brasil Closed group	27	members
			BMW Brasil Closed Group	3	members
			BMW-BMW Brasil MOTOCICLISMO Open group	1	members
			BMW Motorrad GD Brasil Open group	1	members

RUSSIA					
	Vkontakte	**584 results found**			
		BMW - не просто АВТО Item		16.778	followers
		BMW Show		9.265	followers
		I ♥ bmw power		7.895	followers
		BMW™		4.955	followers
		BMW X5 (official page)		4.847	followers
		BMW M GmbH		3.788	followers
		BMW M Power		2.915	followers
		BMW		2.906	followers
		BMW Deutsch Stil		2.677	followers
		BMW		1.675	followers
			5,444 results found		
			BMW Open Group	102.525	members
			BMW Open Group	72.924	members
			BMW ФАН-КЛУБ Open Group	36.223	members
			~"*°•. BMW Style .•°*"~ Closed Group	34.269	members
			BMW-это сила.!.!.!.!.! Open Group	12.893	members
			BMW>>>БМВ>>>BMW>>>БМВ>>>BMW>>> Closed Group	10.383	members
			BMW - racing club Open Group	6.756	members
			BMW#1 Closed Group	6.535	members
			BMW Club Open Group	6.165	members
			BMW E30 Open Group	5.406	members
INDIA	-				
	Facebook	**19 results found**			
		BMW India Cars		359.596	likes
		BMW Motorrad India -Navnit Group		19.433	likes

		BMW India Non-profit organisation		301	likes
		BMW Fan Club: India		150	likes
		BMW India by Infinity Automotive		113	likes
		BMW India Automobiles and parts		85	likes
		BMW Club of India (Proposed) Non-Profit Organisation		61	likes
		BMW Plant Chennai India Product/Services		12	likes
		BMW India Cars		12	likes
		BMW India		2	likes
			15 results found		
			Indians 1974 BMW R90S Open Group	1.856	members
			BMW GROUP INDIA Open Group	177	members
			BMW owners club of India Open Group	80	members
			Indianapolis BMW Club Closed Group	62	members
			BMW INDIA Closed Group	38	members
			BMW India Open Group	14	members
			BMW India Owners Open Group	2	members
			BMW INDIA Open Group	1	members
			BMW Club of India	1	members
			Indianapolis BMW Club Closed Group	1	members
<u>**CHINA**</u>					
	RenRen	**73 Results found**			
		宝马中国 - BMW China		20.424	个好友
		宝马3系 BMW		10.22	个好友

		Series 3		0	
		宝马集团 - BMW Group		4.090	个好友
		宝马X6 - BMW 6		1.289	个好友
		菁翼中国梦想之悦		1.016	个好友
		华晨宝马汽车有限公司 - Brilliance BMW		916	个好友
		宝马Z4 - BMW Z4		839	个好友
		BMW宝马 - BMW BMW		800	个好友
		BMW M3 CLUB		122	个好友
		宝马X1 - BMW X1		37	个好友
	Kaixin001	**5 results found**			
		BMW		752.775	位
		燕宝BMW		2.813	位
		BMW JOY 悦行东方		1.437	位
		宝马BMW · 乐部		370	位
		宝马MINI · 乐部		112	位
	SinaWeibo	**<1000 results found**			
		红宝马俱乐部		65.814	粉丝
		宝马BMW中国		45.475	粉丝
		北京燕宝BMW		28.617	粉丝
		BMW官方车主		21.64	粉丝

		俱乐部		6	
		BMW南京宝利丰		11.794	粉丝
		BMW・乐部		7.088	粉丝
		BMW-乔		5.841	粉丝
		北京宝泽行BMW		4.692	粉丝
		BMW武汉鄂宝		4.523	粉丝
		BMWM・乐部		4.504	粉丝

XVI. Results of the Quantitative Analysis – adidas

adidas	08.03.2012				
Country	*Network*	*Page*	*Group*	#	*Description*
BRAZIL					
	Facebook	**20 results found**			
		Adidas do Brasil Community Page		62	likes
		Adidas micoach Brasil Amateur sports team		36	likes
		ADIDAS BRA-SIL Sports Venue		34	likes
		adidas Eyewear Brasil Limeira, Brazil, Outdoor gear/ Sporting goods		21	likes
		Adidas do Brasil Local Business		18	likes
		Adidas do Brasil Local Business		9	likes
		ADiDAS DO BRASIL LTDS Company/ Com-munity Page		5	likes
		Adidas do Brasil. Local Business		5	likes
		Adidas do Brasil		4	likes
		Shop Brasil - Produtos Adidas Originais Cloth-ing		4	likes
			5 results found		
			Adidas do Brasil Closed Group	74	members
			ESCUELA PILOTO NA-CIONES UNIDAS PRO-MOCION 2003 5TO BRA-SIL.Closed Group	27	members
			Hijos de Adidos Brasil 2000 Open Group	15	members

			ADIDAS, please SPONSOR BRASIL FOOTBALL TEAM(Nike has horrible shirts) Open Group	4	members
			Yo pertenecí a la Asociación de Auxiliares de Adidos en Brasil Open Group	4	members
RUSSIA					
	Vkontakte	**1.147 results found**			
		Adidas		25.991	followers
		Adidas Originals® |BRAND WITH THREE STRIPES| Item		15.088	followers
		Adidas_Discount Center_Липецк-Линия Sports Organization		7.167	followers
		I ♥ Adidas Sport		5.538	followers
		▌▌▌ adidas ▌▌ ▌Club		4.345	followers
		Картинки adidas Website		4.296	followers
		▌▌▌ like adidas™ ▌▌▌ Club		3.998	followers
		Adidas Wheels		2.223	followers
		Adidas		1.767	followers
		★★★<<< ツadidas ツspoRT >>>★★★		1.246	followers
			17.168 results found		
			adidas Sport Open Group	390.731	members
			Adidas / / / Originals Open Group	133.535	members
			adidas Originals Open Group	133.298	members
			Adidas Open Group	21.365	members

			♕ /// ADIDAS /// ♕ Closed Group	17.951	members
			Adidas [GraFFITi] Open Group	11.012	members
			Adidas (Адидас)Open Group	3.802	members
			adidas Россия Open Group	2.804	members
			Адидас(adidas),,,,,,,,,,,,,,,,,,,,,,, Open Group	2.787	members
			[ADIDAS] Open Group	2.566	members
INDIA					
	Facebook	**13 results found**			
		Adidas India Company		895	likes
		adidas India Local business		429	likes
		A_S_I_D_A_S = A Dirty Indian Did A Shit Local business		262	likes
		adidas Running India Company		254	likes
		Adidas India Inc.		47	likes
		Adidas India Company		46	likes
		adidas football India Company		41	likes
		Adidas India Clothing		21	likes
		adidas India Marketing PVT. Ltd.		21	likes
		adidas india Company Community Page		12	likes
			1 result found		
			"The adistar - Ex adidas India Team" Closed group	106	members
CHINA					
	RenRen	**105 results found**			
		阿迪达斯三叶草		362.230	个好友
		阿迪达斯足球		165.1	个好友

				57	
		adidas NEO		3.720	个好友
		阿迪达斯		2.233	个好友
		阿迪达斯adidas		976	个好友
		阿迪达斯adidas		976	个好友
		NIKE&adidas		879	个好友
		阿迪达斯经典三叶草		122	个好友
		联合梦想公司		75	个好友
		耐克和阿迪达斯		3	个好友
	Kaixin001	**1 result found**			
		阿迪达斯		69.302	位
	SinaWeibo	**>1000 results found**			
		阿迪达斯篮球		142.452	粉丝
		阿迪达斯足球		83.567	粉丝
		阿迪达斯跑▪		57.566	粉丝
		阿迪达斯训练		42.464	粉丝
		阿迪达斯官方旗舰店		10.924	粉丝
		泰勒梅阿迪达斯高尔夫		7.024	粉丝
		佳佳-阿迪达斯正品折扣店		4.439	粉丝
		阿迪达斯在中国		3.502	粉丝
		阿迪达斯招聘 - adidas recruiting		3.407	粉丝
		爱尚阿迪达斯		2.526	粉丝

XVII. Results of the Quantitative Analysis – NIVEA

NIVEA	08.03.2012				
Country	*Network*	*Page*	*Group*	#	*Description*
BRAZIL					
	Facebook	**2 results found**			
		Nivea Brasil Health/ Beauty		190.7 69	likes
		NIVEA-BRASILIANA Local Business		2	likes
			0 results found		
RUSSIA					
	Vkontakte	**7 results found**			
		Nivea		2	follower
		NIVEA - ваше счастье и красота…Item		2	follower
		Уход за кожей лица NIVEA VISAGE YOUNG Уход для		2	follower
		Nivea Item		1	follower
		Дезодорант "NIVEA"-невидемая защита		0	follower
		NIVEA		0	follower
			78 results found		
			NIVEA Lip Care: улыбайся, влюбляйся, целуйся!	619.4 44	members
			ВСЕ ДЛЯ ВАШЕЙ КОЖИ И ВОЛОС ♥ L'OREAL ♥ GARNIER ♥ NIVEA ♥ Closed Group	977	members
			Школа Популярности. NIVEA Angel Star Open Group	481	members
			Yes! и Nivea Angel Star выбирают Идеальную	100	members

			девушку Closed Group		
			Стань звездой с Nivea Visage! Open Group	76	members
			<<<<*NIVEA Lip Care*>>>> Open Group	57	members
			Помады и блески для губ Nivea. Open Group	43	members
			Nivea супер-КОНКУРС)) Open Group	28	members
			NIVEA красота это уверенность Open Group	28	members
			NIVEA PROMO Open Group	19	members
INDIA					
	Facebook	**5 results found**			
		NIVEAIndia		216.331	likes
		Nivea India Health/Beauty		55	likes
		Nivea India Health/Beauty		4	likes
		Nivea India LTD Health/Beauty		6	likes
		NIVEA INDIA PVT LTD Company Community Page		22	likes
		Nivea India		3	likes
			2 results found		
			NIVEA India Open group	2	members
			W dzieciństwie malowałem/łam symbole indiańskie na twarzy kremem nivea. Open group	1	members
CHINA					
	RenRen	**1 result found**			
		NIVEA男士调查局		5	个好友
	Kaixin	**1 result found**			
		妮维雅		34.983	位
	SinaWeibo	**> 500 results**	2 groups have about 20000		

		found	fans together		
		NI- VEA妮维雅官方		18.74 5	粉丝
		妮维雅微博		10.32 4	粉丝

XVIII. User Survey

Social Media Marketing at BMW, adidas and NIVEA in Social Networking Sites of the BRIC Countries

Question 1: What is your country of Origin?

- Brazil
- Russia
- India
- China

Question 2: Which social network(s) are you using?

- *Facebook*
- *Orkut*
- В Контакте (VKontakte)
- • 心网 (Kaixin001)
- 人人网 (Renren)
- 新浪微博 (Sina Weibo)

Question 3: You are considering the following brand:

- BMW
- adidas
- NIVEA

Question 4: Concerning your personal engagement, how often do you comment on the page?

- Never
- 1-5
- 6-10
- >10
- if> 10: ___
-

Question 5: How do you evaluate the social media appearance of the chosen brand?

- 1 Very Good
- 2 Good
- 3 Average
- 4 Below Average
- 5 Poor

Question 6: Which of the following marketing approaches does the firm use within the social network?

- Use of local language
- Use of nationals in advertisement (e.g. local people, models, etc.)

- Use of local traditions (e.g. Carnival of Rio, Chinese New Year, etc.)
- Use of famous national sights your country (e.g. Indian Taj Mahal, Russian Kremlin, etc.)
- Use of German traditions in advertisement (e.g. Beer drinking, Sauerkraut, Oktoberfest, etc.)
- Use of German sights (e.g. Berlin, Neuschwanstein, Bavarian Images, etc.)
- None
- Other approaches

Question 7: How active is the brand in marketing/ advertisement within the social network?

- 1 Very active
- 2 Active
- 3 Average
- 4 Not really active
- 5 Not active at all

Question 8: Do you think the brand could engage more in this Network?

- Yes
- No

Question 9: Do you think the company should…

- adapt its advertisement more to your country
- design a more international approach
- stay with its recent approach

Question 10: Do you have suggestions for improvement?

- More engagement with users
- More product information
- More news about the brand
- More job recruitment
- More games and lotteries
- Less general posts
- Less product information
- Less news about the brand
- Less job recruitment
- Less games and lotteries
- Other suggestions